WINNING WAYS FOR BUSINESS IN EUROPE

This book is dedicated to my mother, Patricia Foster

WINNING WAYS FOR BUSINESS IN EUROPE

Top Business Leaders Discuss their Strategies for the New Europe

Compiled and Edited by
TIMOTHY R V FOSTER

KOGAN PAGE

First published in 1993

Apart from any fair dealing for the purposes of research or private study, or criticism or review, as permitted under the Copyright, Designs and Patents Act, 1988, this publication may only be reproduced, stored or transmitted, in any form or by any means, with the prior permission in writing of the publishers, or in the case of reprographic reproduction in accordance with the terms of licences issued by the Copyright Licensing Agency. Enquiries concerning reproduction outside those terms should be sent to the publishers at the undermentioned address:

Kogan Page Limited
120 Pentonville Road
London N1 9JN

© Timothy R V Foster, 1993

British Library Cataloguing in Publication Data

A CIP record for this book is available from the British Library.

ISBN 0 7494 1055 8

Typeset by Photoprint, Torquay, Devon
Printed and bound in Great Britain by Biddles Ltd, Guildford and Kings Lynn

Contents

Introduction 7
Timothy R V Foster

1 Chemicals 11
Strategy for doing business in central and
eastern Europe
*David V S Williamson, President, Europe,
Du Pont de Nemours International SA, Geneva*

2 Communications and public affairs 21
Communications consultancy in transition
*James B Lindheim, Chairman,
Burson-Marsteller Europe, Paris*

3 Computers 31
Putting flexibility and speed to work
*Theo Lieven, Chairman,
Vobis Microcomputer AG, Aachen*

4 Contract catering 43
Catering for Europe
*Garry Hawkes, Chief Executive,
Gardner Merchant Services Group, London*

5 Courier services 53
The challenges ahead in courier services
*Robert M Kuijpers, Chief Executive Officer,
Europe/Africa,
DHL Worldwide Express, Brussels*

6 Foods 63
Managing change in manufacturing organisations
*Edward S Moerk, President,
Campbell Biscuits Europe, Brussels*

7	**Hotels and restaurants** Developing an international network of branded hotels and restaurants *Rocco Forte, Chairman,* *Forte PLC*	71
8	**Information technology** Trends in the European information technology services market *Vernon Ellis, Managing Partner, Europe,* *Andersen Consulting, London*	81
9	**Payment systems** Common knowledge *Charles T Russell, President,* *Visa International, San Francisco*	97
10	**'Mirror, mirror, on the wall' . . . Pharmaceuticals** Shaping the image of the pharmaceutical industry *Henry Wendt, Chairman,* *SmithKline Beecham PLC, London*	107
11	**Property** The future of the real estate market *Stuart Lipton, Chief Executive,* *Stanhope Properties PLC, London*	121
12	**Sporting apparel** It's not just shoes! *John Duerden, President,* *Reebok International Division, London*	133
Index		**145**

Introduction

The twelve contributors to this book are all chief executives or chairmen of some of the world's leading corporations. I asked them to give their observations, vision and experience about how they are, or are planning to be, running their businesses for the rest of the century, with particular emphasis on their strategies for Europe. Their thinking makes fascinating reading, and I would like to acknowledge all the executives and their staffs who helped make this book possible.

Some of the concepts that are repeated time and again in these short treatises are:

- We are living in an era of accelerating change. Things will never be the same. The way businesses are being managed recognises this. But businesses must be prepared to adapt often to meet change. The 'future' (where things are different) is as near as six months away in some cases, leading to a strategy of speed and flexibility.
- Corporate rationalisation, simplification, cost reduction, management delayering, outsourcing, multiskilling, organisational re-engineering and flexibility enhancement are all buzzwords in full flight in these pages.
- Most of the companies here aspire to be world-class leaders by the end of the century (if they are not already). Their strategies are aimed at achieving and maintaining this goal. Most of them see their playing field as the world.
- Customer awareness and expectations are higher than ever. Quality is critically important. Failure to address these aspects means failure to survive. Continuous improvement (kaizen) is a very popular strategy.
- It is thus essential to focus on the customer's needs. Getting closer to the customer, paying attention to detail, are key strategies for many. Automation, technology and communications are tools that enable these activities.

- Relationships with customers are becoming less adversarial. Partnering with customers and suppliers is the trend. Win/win is the desired result. And results, not process, are what count.
- The strength of the brand is paramount. Several companies have reduced the number of their brands so that they can apply their full resources on the strongest brands in their portfolios. Power branding or niche management make up the focus, so that a very clear proposition can be offered to the target customer and a simplification of the message can be made.
- In spite of all the promise of global strategies, pan-European communications and the removal of trade and other cross-border barriers, there are still a whole lot of diverse cultures out there that demand to be recognised. 'Think global, act local' is a well-worn phrase that is very applicable.
- Government regulations are still getting in the way of progress. Harmonisation and standardisation of regulations and specifications yet have a long way to go in many areas.

OPTIMISM PREVAILS

Most the companies covered in this book feel that they have an enormous opportunity in the next decade. In spite of obvious maturity in some markets, they feel that their strategies will work in delivering on their expectations. Here is a brief and promising summary:

DuPont (chemicals) sees oncoming sustained economic prosperity in Europe being a driver of a bright future.

Burson-Marsteller (communications and public affairs) sees the growing recognition by European business of the importance of communications, as well as the development of niche markets that it is uniquely qualified to serve, as major opportunities.

Vobis (computers) believes its strategy of speed and flexibility, served by its superb inventory management system, will make it the European computer firm most responsive to customer needs.

Gardner Merchant (contract catering) heralds privatisation, the opening up of state organisations to private enterprise and event catering as being powerful contributors to its future growth.

DHL (courier services) believes the increasing trend to just-in-time delivery and the globalisation of resources and standards will increase demand for fast small-package delivery.

Campbell Biscuits Europe (foods) believes that there will only be three major pan-European biscuit manufacturers left after the turn of the century, and expects to be one of these, based on its vision and strategies.

Forte Plc (hotels and restaurants) looks at the relative lack of hotels and restaurants owned by multiple operators in Europe as very promising.

Andersen Consulting (information technology) sees itself as 'a transnational organisation founded on national partnerships, bound together into an internationally integrated and interdependent firm'. In this way it enjoys natural synergy so that it can deliver what is needed by its clients in the great variety of ways required.

Visa International (payment systems) sees travellers and cross-border payments as the wedge market to a transparent new world of transactions that measures up to 'about US$8 trillion'.

SmithKline Beecham (pharmaceuticals) calls for its industry to work hard at correcting its image problems by enhancing communications with its publics and partnering with the rest of the healthcare sector, leading to 'new heights of social and financial performance'.

Stanhope (property) believes its orientation towards the customer and focus on quality and cost-effectiveness will help lead it out of the malaise suffered by its industry.

Reebok (sporting apparel) sees its global branding strategy as key to its future success, in a marketplace where it expects branded sports clothing to double the branded footwear business, which is already at $26 billion retail.

I have gathered together 12 of the leading businesses in the world in a variety of disciplines to report on *Winning Ways for Business in Europe*. I hope that the information will prove valuable, if not inspirational, to all who count the success of business as important to their future.

1
Chemicals

Strategy for Doing Business in Central and Eastern Europe

David V S Williamson
President, Europe,
Du Pont de Nemours International SA

I suspect there has never been an observer of history who has concluded that he lives in predictable and uninteresting times. There is a natural tendency to exaggerate the importance of current events, and so each generation imagines itself at some historic crossroads. However, I believe these truly are extraordinary times. In the space of just a few years, dramatic changes have reshaped world politics and economies, and often we in Europe have found ourselves on centre stage.

The changes in eastern and central Europe – unfolding every day – are familiar to us all and I offer no expert insight. But consider also what is happening in western Europe, where decades of incremental progress in the European Community have accelerated into a race toward – and beyond – the EC 1992 initiatives. In addition to considering a deepening of their commitments to each other, Community members are also trying to broaden their view to include a wider European Economic Area, and in the longer-term an even larger and more unified European marketplace that can be a major player in . . .

. . . A 'NEW WORLD ORDER'

These developments have had a major effect on companies like my own. Investment has increased, and so have mergers, acquisitions, divestitures and joint ventures as companies re-evaluate their business portfolios in a bigger and more unified market. At the same time, particularly during today's difficult economic times, there has been a strong emphasis on cost reductions, as companies seek to remain profitable and competitive in a more crowded field. As a result of these and other developments, industry has been asked to face up to tough problems, including growing concern about job security and the very serious challenge of improved environmental protection.

Although historically an American company, DuPont is becoming truly global, and with a third of our business in Europe, we are thoroughly familiar with these issues. We have stepped up investment in Europe and have clearly defined this region as a major growth market. We continuously evaluate our businesses, looking for opportunities to improve our strategic position. We are currently engaged in a very significant restructuring programme that will further enhance our ability to offer superior value to customers.

IN SPITE OF CHALLENGES

DuPont has confronted difficult problems related to environmental protection, cost competitiveness and job security for its employees – problems shared by much of European industry. In the environmental arena, we have acknowledged serious problems in both the manufacture and use of our products, but we have also established an aggressive improvement programme, and we have advanced the view that outstanding environmental performance should be viewed not as an unwanted or costly nuisance, but as a business opportunity that will result in long-term reward. Similarly, we have learned to value simplified ways of operating our businesses, enriching the job satisfaction of our employees while dealing sensitively with individuals who have to leave as we learn to operate with leaner teams.

HOW, THEN, TO PARTICIPATE?

These major challenges and exciting opportunities help shape the broad view of western companies in today's climate. For companies like DuPont, the question then becomes, how can we best participate in the unfolding social and economic progress of eastern and central Europe? Because we are a global company, we seek to involve the talents and capabilities of people and markets everywhere we reasonably can. But in this region, as in all others, we want to do so in a committed way, by becoming members of a social partnership rather than opportunistic traders. The issue is how and when.

There is no question that private business must be a key partner in building a strong market economy in eastern and central Europe. The failure of state-run economic systems has underlined the fact that private enterprise systems are best equipped to provide the goods and services necessary to achieve sustained prosperity. Private companies are the organisations prepared to bring together the human and technical resources with the flexibility and market expertise needed in the region.

Although some important investments have been made in Hungary, the Czech Republic, Poland and Russia, by comparison with western countries they are modest and do not include the chemical area. Let me illustrate some reasons why, by citing the example of my own company. DuPont is a large global company, with sales of about $38 billion. Our principal businesses are chemicals, polymers, fibres and specialty products, as well as petroleum exploration, production, refining and marketing. Each year we make capital investments of about $5 billion, and since we operate in 60 countries, investments are made all around the world every day.

In Russia, for example, Conoco, DuPont's energy subsidiary, formed at the end of 1991 as a 50–50 joint venture with a Russian enterprise to develop an oil field in the Timan Pechora basin west of the Urals and close to the Arctic Circle. With recoverable reserves estimated at 110 million barrels, the 'Polar Lights' venture is scheduled to start production in late 1994.

In the Czech Republic, Hungary and Poland, networks of filling and service stations are being established and investment in one or more refineries is being evaluated.

DuPont established its first presence in eastern and central Europe with an office in Moscow in 1974 and one in Warsaw a year later. Following the political upheaval and economic changes in 1989, DuPont has moved to build up its presence with subsidiaries in virtually all countries; the company thus has the infrastructure in place to take investment decisions at the appropriate time.

INVESTMENT CRITERIA

How do we determine where to spend our capital resources? Clearly we have more good ideas than money to support them. So we have developed criteria to help us prioritise potential investments in new locations. These criteria apply to all countries and regions, and they are designed to help us balance business opportunities with risk and uncertainty. What do we look for?

- The overall economics of the investment should be attractive, without impediments to repatriation of earnings so that we can reward the shareholders.

- The business climate should allow us to operate safely and ethically, valuing our people and protecting the environment.

- We should feel welcome, both nationally and locally.

- Good quality people should be available in adequate numbers.

- A sound infrastructure for power supplies, transportation, communications and similar services should be in place or about to be installed.

- The legal and governmental framework should limit risk and facilitate business. Laws governing investment and property ownership must be clear. Vague assurances on these points are not enough. We prefer national laws that permit 100 per cent ownership of the equity even though we may operate with a partner. It is helpful if a single governmental authority is responsible for negotiating conditions and permits.

- When we are evaluating new commitments in unfamiliar parts of the world, we look for ways to reduce perceived risks which may be legal and political as well as business related. Investment grants and tax incentives, or other ways of balancing unusual cost or risk, may be appropriate.

HOW THESE CRITERIA CAN BE MET

In the past, countries in eastern and central Europe had a difficult time meeting these criteria, and as a result, they did not attract significant investment from companies like DuPont. Even today, we understand that some of these criteria – particularly financial incentives – are very difficult for central and eastern European governments to meet. However, there are still actions those governments can take to attract investment:

- They can study laws and practices in parts of the European Community and among Pacific rim countries to understand how they attract private investment.
- They can create development boards to bring together all the financial and technical specialists needed to negotiate with companies.
- They can look for other creative ways to encourage investment.

Fundamentally, their goal should be to become globally competitive in the battle for private investment. To do this, they should seek to minimise any excessive risk private companies must face. Companies like DuPont want increased presence in eastern Europe, but have more good opportunities around the world than money to invest. They make decisions balancing the potential for financial success with risk for their shareholders.

A WESTERN CONTRIBUTION

I also believe western governments can help protect private companies from excessive risk, thereby encouraging more rapid development in the region. Their interest in doing so should be readily apparent.

First, from a strategic point of view, western governments have a major interest in contributing to strong and stable economies in the region. The events of 1992–93 opened the doors to change, but they did not usher in an era of universal peace and stability. If there is to be a 'new world order' it must begin with nations and regions that enjoy strong economies and growing prosperity.

Second, guarantees to encourage private investment are far more cost-effective than traditional foreign aid. In the current political climate, western governments are reluctant to make large foreign-aid commitments at the expense of domestic programmes. Partnership with private companies is a far more attractive – and more effective – route.

Third, growing prosperity in eastern and central Europe, based on a market economy, offers the potential for vastly expanded trade with the West. As markets grow and develop, all regions can profit.

HOW THE WEST CAN HELP

If western governments should join in a new partnership, the question then becomes, how can they best do so? Once again, the answer lies in helping to protect private companies from excessive risk. Investments could be guaranteed against political risk at no cost.

As a further example, western investors could be provided with interest-free loans, with the interest paid from foreign-aid budgets. This could mean that $10 billion of foreign aid per year could be leveraged into $100 billion per year of private investments. And as a rule of thumb, every job created directly by a foreign investor creates another three to five jobs to support the required infrastructure. These investments would also bring modern technologies and business methods to the region.

Western governments could also serve as catalysts by offering a multi-year tax moratorium on repatriated earnings. This would definitely make investments more attractive and accelerate economic development.

THE IMPLICATIONS OF STRONGER PARTNERSHIPS BETWEEN GOVERNMENT AND INDUSTRY

If the various governments and private companies form stronger partnerships, what specifically can this mean in practical terms for the region?

This is from DuPont's perspective, but I believe that our point of view is representative of many in industry. Although we have had offices and sales operations in parts of eastern and central Europe for decades, it is fair to say that the region was not generally strategically important to us before the mid-1980s – a place where we sold, but had few long-term commitments. In the latter half of the 1980s, however, our interest increased. We began to regard the region as strategic for several businesses, made more long-term supply agreements, began large-scale purchasing and included eastern Europe in global long-term planning.

Looking ahead, we want our involvement to grow. At the moment, we need to import products and build a strong customer base. We need to get to know each other better and build up our technical, marketing, commercial and communications capability. We need to continue to recruit and train employees from the region so they can take over leadership of our activities in these countries as our presence grows. In fact, we have trained many eastern Europeans in western Europe and the United States. We also provide two MBA scholarships in the USA per year for our most promising employees. In terms of technology, we will be working with local customers to help them make products that are competitive not only here, but throughout Europe and beyond.

HOW TO BUILD PARTNERSHIPS

The routes to increased partnership in the economy are many. Building our presence to serve our customers with technical and marketing advice is low risk and high probability. Increased distribution capability through stocking points and service centres is an obvious step. So are technical centres. Packaging and finishing operations to prepare products for local market needs can be quite sophisticated and are not necessarily small investments. In fact, for some product lines this involves high technology formulating and compounding. In general, these kinds of commitments are appropriate because they meet the short-term needs of the economy quickly.

At the other end of the spectrum of our industry's activities are the production of basic chemicals and petrochemical building blocks. The commonly recognised polymers and similar products that characterise the chemical industry are less likely to be attractive in the short term. To be competitive, such units need to be large and well integrated with raw-material-supply and customer-distribution networks. They are expensive, more risky, and generally less needed in the current situation of adequate global capacity.

There are many other routes as well – including the purchase of, or joint-venturing with, existing assets. These ideas often sound attractive, but we must be sure they fit strategically and that they can be properly integrated into our global operations so that we can ensure their development. We are not a kind of holding company. We want to be able to support and build activities using our core competencies. So when we seek to acquire an interest, we are concerned with the strategic fit as well as with issues like the technology, work practices, environmental liability and ownership. Good fits are relatively rare.

Our preference is for greenfield sites and 100 per cent ownership. Generally our experience with joint ventures is mixed and we find progress is faster if we are allowed to do what we know best.

In general, then, our involvement in eastern and central Europe will increase as we build our co-operation with customers and build resources and presence to support them. Our goal now is to help the area in its development of a market economy – to contribute to growth, help create wealth and jobs, and in the spirit of free markets, to make some money!

OUTLOOK: POSITIVE

Longer term, we see a bright future. We see all of eastern and central Europe integrated into the larger European community. We envisage a time in the not too distant future when the people of this region will enjoy sustained economic prosperity, and we anticipate that DuPont will have an important role in that future, a partner with manufacturing and technical, as well as a business presence . . . an employer . . . a taxpayer . . . a customer as well as a supplier in the community.

David V S Williamson

From 1961 to 1963 Dr Williamson worked as a research chemist with Battelle Memorial Institute. In 1963 he joined Du Pont de Nemours International SA (DISA) in Geneva in marketing activities. After a period as a sales manager in Germany and on special assignment in Wilmington (USA), he returned to Geneva in 1970 and held positions in the Plastics and Material & Logistics Departments. In July 1985 he was named Group Managing Director, Europe, with responsibility for several departments and countries. In July 1989, Dr Williamson was appointed Vice-President for the Europe, Middle East and Africa Region with responsibilities for DuPont's chemicals and specialties activities, and Chairman of DISA. On 1 November 1990 he was named to the position of President, Europe, and on 31 August 1991 he assumed the additional role of Senior Vice President, Agricultural Products. He is the first member of the company's senior management operating group to reside in Europe.

Dr Williamson graduated from the Universities of Aberdeen and Leeds in the United Kingdom with BSc (Honours) and PhD degrees in chemical engineering. In July 1990 he was given the honorary degree of Doctor of Science by the University of Ulster.

E I Du Pont de Nemours and Company

DuPont, the worldwide chemicals, specialties and energy company, makes a major contribution to European economies.

In Europe, the company employs almost 21,000 people in 25 manufacturing plants and more than 20 laboratories and customer service centres across 27 countries.

For 1992, DuPont reported worldwide company sales of $37.8 billion and European sales of $14.2 billion.

The company's principal businesses include: chemicals, fibres, polymers, petroleum and diversified businesses (agricultural products, electronics, imaging systems and medical products). Major markets include: aerospace, apparel, automotive, chemicals, construction, electronics, food, healthcare, printing, paper, refining and transportation.

Conoco, the DuPont petroleum subsidiary, is exploring for oil or natural gas in about 15 countries on five continents. It currently produces petroleum in eight countries on three continents. It markets gasoline in the United States and 13 European countries.

In 1992, DuPont was the eighth largest US industrial corporation (Fortune 500). It was ranked the 22nd largest industrial corporation in the world in 1991 (Fortune Global 500).

2
Communications and Public Affairs

Communications Consultancy in Transition

James B Lindheim
Chairman,
Burson-Marsteller Europe, Paris

Communications consultancy has evolved out of the traditional public relations business – making sure that clients or their products get the kind of publicity that they need to meet their business objectives. Over the years that base has grown within individual European countries to encompass many more services – crisis management and crisis preparedness; marketing programmes that involve trade relations, promotions, cause-marketing, etc; public affairs involving government relations, ally development, community affairs; internal communications involving corporate mission programmes, sales training, and corporate change; financial communications including specialty areas such as acquisitions and privatisations; environmental communications including training of executives in risk communications, etc.

All of these expansions have reflected the growing realisation by business organisations that communications is an important element to achieve basic objectives: selling products and services, building brand equities, gaining public or government permission to build a plant or sell a product, winning the support of investors, or motivating employees to a more competitive and market-focused behaviour.

Like every industry in Europe, communications consultancy finds itself in transition from a highly local, country-based activity to activities which require cross-border co-ordination and delivery. Like many European businesses, Burson-Marsteller's services often were developed locally, driven by the skills and interests of our country managers as well as the peculiarities of the national market and our local managers' sense of where we could gain competitive advantage.

Thus, if one audited the range of services offered by Burson-Marsteller in each European country as of 1988, one might have found very different collections of services offered. In Scandinavia there was a heavy emphasis on corporate communications; in Spain an emphasis on marketing communications; and in the UK we were building an excellent reputation for crisis management. Today, the audit would probably show a much more balanced picture, partially because the markets themselves have become more similar but also clients demanded the transmigration of ideas from one market to the next.

While some believed that the removal of borders as a result of the 1992 programme was going to mean a revolution in our business, we believed otherwise. Communications services in Europe must always be delivered on the ground in what is a national – and sometimes subnational – context.

Clients who want our services in Holland want to know that we know enough about the Dutch market, political scene, media scene, issues and fads that we can effectively impact the ideas and behaviours of Dutch people. Therefore, the 1992 programme did not seem to offer us the possibility to consolidate operations or to deliver Dutch services out of Belgium. Indeed, during the period of 1988–91 we actually increased the number of our localities substantially, adding Barcelona in Spain; Munich, Berlin, and Bonn in Germany; Rome in Italy; Zurich in Switzerland; and adding new countries to our region: Denmark, Hungary, the Czech Republic, and Poland.

We expanded on a national and regional level because it became increasingly obvious that many of our clients were becoming more international. Our original reason to enter the European market in the mid-1960s was to follow our big US clients. By the mid-1980s only about one-third of our business was based on those clients; more and more we had national clients seeking national services or, often, the local national affiliate of a multinational company was hiring us locally, not because we had a relationship back at headquarters in the US or UK, but because we were strong locally.

Starting in the late 1980s, however, the Single Market phenomenon began to generate a new kind of business for us – large European corporations that wanted to conduct marketing programmes or needed to conduct public affairs programmes on a pan-European basis. Thus, we needed to be able to assure that we could offer a truly consistent range of services across borders and that we could network our resources in such a way as to deliver a kind of 'seamlessness' across Europe. Often this was a seamlessness which went way beyond what the client company was able to organise for itself, since many client organisations remained riddled by a feudal structure which prevented the very kind of multi-country co-operation which they knew they needed.

That led us to the creation between 1989 and 1992 of matrix style practice structure to assure that in our key areas of business – marketing, public affairs, health-care communications, and corporate/financial communications – a practice leader in Europe would work with national practice leaders to both develop services in each market and assure a consistent level of quality and approach. Practices were also designed to increase a 'networking' culture within Burson-Marsteller, ie, to assure that account executives felt motivated to use experts around the system in the delivery of the highest quality services to the clients. By 1992 one of the trade publications which publishes an international report card on agencies gave Burson-Marsteller an A+ for its international network, saying that no competitor even came close. That was a reflection of the extensive resources put into this effort over the previous years.

As the European recession unfolded, however, in 1992–93, it became increasingly obvious that the high cost of this effort was eroding margins and not necessarily leading to enough new growth opportunities.

There were, as expected, a steadily growing number of 'international' requests, particularly in the area of marketing communications and issue management, but these were not necessarily capable of eroding a loss of business to price-cutting hungry national competitors who were able to offer strictly national clients a strictly national service, where the advantages of the B-M network were much less obvious and often irrelevant.

Thus, in 1993 we decided to re-examine our assumptions about the marketplace and once again decide how to allocate resources and management for the next three years.

MARKETPLACE STRATEGIES

We continued to believe that the markets we served in Europe would be both international and national. We would have to have a structure and a pricing approach which allowed us to compete with aggressive local competitors who did not have the network cost structure we must continue to have. And we had to assure that our international structure remained uniquely strong and effective so that no other competitor could match it. This required several things:

1. The basics of the business had to be sound, particularly media relations, which remains for many clients the bedrock criterion of what public relations and communications consultancies are about.
2. There had to be greater pricing flexibility and new ways to price and deliver services. In several countries we eliminated hours-based billing and reinstituted the old way of pricing, ie, retainer or flat-fee arrangements. We also started to provide our professionals on a part-time or full-time secondment to clients, recognising that often it is the expertise on the ground which is needed rather than the full agency at an arm's length relationship. We have also explored opportunities for value-based billing, particularly in the areas of financial communications and government relations. How much is success worth to a client? That can be the basis for the value of the service provided.
3. We recognised that we had to aggressively pursue market niches where we were able, because of our greater knowledge and professionalism versus the local competition; to offer services which they could not offer, at least for several months or years. This was the story of our success in the crisis management area, where we led the market for several years in various European countries. Market niching required that we increase our market sensitivity and be creative about the development of new services which met needs that other competitors had no way of identifying or meeting.
4. The market itself had to be expanded and we as an industry leader had to actively pursue that end. Communications remains for most European managers an afterthought and a mysterious if not nerve-wracking area. Most European busi-

ness schools do not teach communications as a basic management function nor do most corporations consider rotation through the communications group a normal part of management development. There was clearly a need to change these perceptions and to help build the marketplace for communications services by educating business management about its criticality to success.

OPERATIONAL STRATEGIES

In order to implement these marketplace strategies, we determined in 1993 a variety of operational strategies for the mid-1990s:

1. *Networking*: We had to increasingly make available to our European offices a technological capability for effective networking. For many years, our cultural bias towards using resources across the network succeeded heroically against an antiquated technological capability to do so. Simple networking technologies had to be implemented along with the appropriate collection of central databanks of information and references. In addition, the practice structures had to be streamlined and updated so that the European practice leader became less of a guru and more of a coach of national practice leaders who themselves generated and transmitted knowledge for both client service and for business development.
2. *Quality*: A study on the subject of quality management and how it might apply in our business concluded that quality starts with an intense client focus. Thus, we launched a quality programme which started with client audits to determine the business needs of clients and to identify how a communications consultancy could best serve those needs. The results of these audits have been used to correct and redirect many client relationships as well as identify areas where our business basics must be improved and where new market niches can be created. They have also been used as a basis for our training programmes to assure that our people are becoming more and more client-centred and client-focused.
3. *Marketing*: A major new marketing effort was launched with several objectives. The first was to differentiate from nationally based agencies, showing how the network operation of

Burson-Marsteller created a superior capacity to produce results in the local market. The second was to build the market for communications consultancy in general, particularly during recessionary times, by discussing the criticality of communications to business success.
4. *Training*: Despite budgetary pressures, training remains a crucial operational strategy. Both local and regional training programmes were implemented, including an annual European-wide training programme (The Burson Academy) to assure that middle management maintained a common approach to key disciplines, understood business-development techniques and also knew each other personally for better networking and resource sharing.
5. *Product development*: Various multi-country teams began to work together to develop new service offerings to clients. In several instances this was a case of taking a product already developed in an individual market and modifying it for broader European use. In other instances, new products were introduced by what was effectively a European brand manager.
6. *Broader management structure*: Until 1992, the European structure of B-M involved a single European CEO to whom reported all the individual Country Managers and the Practice Leaders. A new structure was created with a more powerful Board consisting of the same individuals and with more of the Board members taking broader responsibilities, eg, for several countries or for basic management functions such as information technology, professional development, budgeting, etc. The objective of this structure was to assure that more of these leaders gained a European perspective and a true international capability and also to assure that the next group of national leaders would get the opportunity to lead.

We continue to believe that our European clients in the 1990s are in the midst of radical change – in their markets, in their political, regulatory and issue problems, and in their structures. This, we believe, creates new opportunities for our services but at the same time heightens the questions of value and results of what we do. As our clients change, so must we, which is why the Burson Quality Programme is based on intense listening to clients in order to understand the areas where we can offer the highest value. As we have followed European clients from multinationalism to a qualified transnationalism we will follow them into the business and political challenges of the mid-1990s which, we believe, will require the highest levels of flexibility and acute attention to the underlying business value of what we offer.

James B Lindheim

Jim Lindheim joined Burson-Marsteller in 1981, serving in senior account management and as Director of the Corporate Services Group. Under his leadership from 1985 to 1988, B-M's Washington office substantially enlarged and deepened its government-relations and constituency-relations capabilities. He moved to B-M/Europe in 1988 as Director of Corporate Services, consulting with clients on a wide range of political, government and social policy issues. He then became Director of Public Affairs for B-M worldwide, based in Paris, heading the Public Affairs Network, a group of global issue experts working with clients on national and international policy challenges including crisis management, preparedness planning and training, constituency relations and risk communications. He was named Chairman of B-M Europe in 1992.

Prior to joining B-M, he was Senior VP and Director of Corporate Priorities Services at the survey research firm of Yankelovich, Skelly and White, Inc., and earlier served as a Research Associate at the consulting firm of Mathematica, Inc. and as Assistant Dean of the Woodrow Wilson School of Public and International Affairs, Princeton University.

He is a *summa cum laude* graduate of Williams College and holds a masters degree in public and international affairs from Princeton.

Burson-Marsteller

Burson-Marsteller is the world's leading communications (public relations/public affairs) consultancy.

B-M is well established in Europe, with over 30 years of experience there, and 630 people in 22 offices in 15 countries, ranking it within the top three firms in most locations. Offices are situated in: Barcelona, Berlin, Bonn, Brussels, Budapest, Copenhagen, Frankfurt, Geneva, Hamburg, London, Madrid, Milan, Moscow, Munich, Oslo, Paris, Prague, Rome, Stockholm, The Hague, Warsaw and Zurich.

B-M's global network includes offices in North and South America, Asia and Australia.

Specific disciplines include:

- marketing communications;
- corporate communications;
- employee communications;
- government relations;
- activist relations;
- crisis preparedness and management,
- third-party communications; and
- media relations.

Burson-Marsteller is part of the Young & Rubicam Group.

3
Computers
Putting Flexibility and Speed to Work
Theo Lieven
Chairman,
Vobis Microcomputer AG, Aachen, Germany

Vobis is the largest personal computer (PC) retailer in Europe. We have over 200 branches in Germany, The Netherlands, Belgium, Italy, Austria, Spain, Luxembourg, Poland, France and Switzerland. We also manufacture our own systems under the Highscreen brand. In 1992, we outsold IBM PCs in Germany two-to-one – a total of 320,000 Highscreen PCs were sold in that year, making us number one. We have 16 per cent of the market in Germany. Our turnover in 1992 was DM 1.5 billion, up 53 per cent on 1991 and our 1992 profits were DM 60 million before tax.

FLEXIBILITY AND SPEED

Flexibility and speed are the words that define our organisation. Flexibility and speed belong together. With low speed you cannot be flexible. In fact, I hear that there are two kinds of company, the speedy, fast ones and the dead!

What do I mean by speed? It's how fast you can react to the needs of the marketplace and deliver what is wanted. Speed is of the essence.

The future is very close in our business, maybe six months away. We don't need five years to design a new product, as they seem to in the car business. A computer takes six or nine months for most manufacturers, and far less for us. As soon as the parts are available we buy them in small quantities, put them together and see how the new design works in the marketplace.

Introducing a new computer

It goes like this. A new development evolves in computer hardware, perhaps a new CPU (central processing unit) chip, an improved LCD (liquid crystal display) screen or a better high-density hard disk drive. Let us say it will be ready for shipment from the far east in nine months' time. Computer manufacturers see an opportunity for a new product based on this improvement, say a refined notebook computer. So they put their ideas together and start the process of new-product development.

IBM might need a lead time of nine months to develop and introduce the new computer; they have to start buying the components immediately. Compaq might need only three months lead time, so they can start buying in six months time. And they get maybe a 20 per cent better price for the components than IBM. We at Vobis need only three weeks lead time! We start buying in eight months, and we get maybe a 30 per cent better price than IBM when they started.

It seems like Vobis is always cheaper than the others. But we are not cheaper: we are faster, we are closer to the market. It is one of our secret ingredients.

Being close to the customer

One of the most important aspects of our business *is* that we are so very close to the end user today. Our inventory control system is one of the most sophisticated you will ever see. With a new product, we give all our stores about two or three units, so we need just a few hundred examples of the product. We run an advertisement, then see what happens. We know after one day whether it is a hit. We can then order the next shipment or just stop it. This is the key success of Vobis. It is the unique advantage of our flexibility and speed.

THE BURGER KING OF COMPUTER RETAILING ('HAVE IT YOUR WAY!')

We offer a greater variety of computers in our retail stores than anybody. It is easy for us because the end of the assembly line of our own brand is in our shops, not the factory. For example, for our current notebook computer we have five different CPU chips, six RAM (random access memory) chips, four hard disk drives, ten keyboards and three types of display screen. We can create hundreds of variations of notebook in this way, with fewer than 30 different items in inventory.

As a customer, you can easily decide in the store what configuration you want, so you can 'have it your way' (as Burger King says) using the desired components. We can provide counselling, if needed, to identify what is most appropriate to the customer's needs. The whole process of customised assembly takes about five minutes. By stocking the components rather than the completed computers, it means we can cut down on inventory and still deliver a superior, tailored product that fits the customer's needs exactly.

We then have our final check in front of the customer. We switch it on, install the operating system and the customer sees it working. We don't sell closed boxes of our own brand.

This flexibility contributes to our success. Each shop has about two engineers. The salesperson works out what the customer wants, and in the few minutes it takes to assemble the finished computer, they can talk about software. Every customer wants different software. We install the software on their hard disk drive while they wait. We offer four different operating systems: MS/DOS, Novell/DR-DOS IBM OS/2 and Unix.

The customers are not necessarily aware of this tailored assembly process. Their perception is that we offer a huge variety of computers. When they realise that we always have it in stock, thanks to our assembly process and super inventory control, that they can walk in, place the order and walk out a few minutes later with precisely what they want, all at a very competitive price, they are very pleased.

ADVERTISING STRATEGY

We spend 4.5 per cent of our total sales budget on advertising – for 1993 that's DM 70 million. After salaries, it is the largest expenditure for the company. I agree with the old adage, 'only half of my advertising is effective, but I don't know which half!' We typically advertise in colour brochures which we insert in newspapers. We also run billboards and straight print ads. I liken what we do to that kind of epoxy glue that comes in two parts. The two components won't glue anything on their own, but when they are combined, they are effective. So it is with our advertising.

We are doing 25,000 billboards for 20 days in July. Every year we do this. They show one or two products so you can remember them very easily, and then you will see the same product in the brochures that are included in your newspaper.

The first two pages of the brochure are normally the theme of the month, one subject that is discussed, as in a computer magazine, and not just from our point of view. We describe how it works, the advantages, the disadvantages and this information helps people. I still write this copy. That was the way when the company was smaller, but why should I stop doing things I know I can do? There are CEO's of air transport companies still flying aeroplanes! It is not necessary to stop!

A typical campaign will run no more than three months, so we don't have the luxury of testing the advertising in advance. We see the results in the stores immediately, that is the test. If we spent a lot of time researching, after we have studied it all, the product will be obsolete, so it makes no sense.

Business people today are often afraid to make decisions. In this business, they know the product this month will be cheaper next month or better for the same price. So they buy only what they need now. That's another reason why flexibility and speed are so important to us.

THE CURRENT BUSINESS OPPORTUNITY

As a mass-market retailer, our biggest challenge is to find good products in the US $100 to $1000 price range. This is where most of the money is. All the hi-fi business is in this range, and TVs too. Anybody will spend $100–$200 for something good that can be thought of as useful.

I think one advance that will be very successful will be the CD photo system that Kodak has introduced, where you take your roll of film into a service bureau, they process the film and put the images on a CD ROM disk. Then you can play them back through your computer, enlarge them, edit them, change the colour, manipulate them and print them. We placed a small advertisement on this and started selling 200 a day. Customers just needed software and a CD-ROM drive. We offered a special deal on the drive with the software. There are already 50 photo-CD processing machines, which cost $300,000 each, in bureaux throughout Europe.

We recently introduced our new electronic organiser, designed by Luigi Colani. It is not yet an image product but Colani is well known in most of Europe and Japan as a designer. The unit is called the Highscreen Colani Organiser. It is useful and a nice product. It gives you a translator in eight languages, even Japanese. It's not very powerful but it has a phone book, a schedule, and it is very cheap at about $120. It even has an alarm clock. It has 128K (kilobytes) of RAM. It was going to be 32K, but everybody has 32K, and 128K was only $7 more and it delivers four times the performance.

DIFFERENTIATION

Another problem in our business (except perhaps for Apple) is differentiation. Everything is compatible, every machine has the same performance, any machine may cost roughly the same, the difference is not so big.

We needed something to differentiate us from others and the only thing we could do was the choice of software we bundled with it, Microsoft Word, Excel, Power Point and so on. After a while everybody did that, so it is not a major advantage anymore. So that brought us to design. Maybe the cosmetics of the item are a consideration. If it looks more individual, nicer, that could make a difference. The second thing is ergonomics. That makes a difference too. We have asked Luigi Colani to design our entire Highscreen line. The results are apparent. The line is beautiful.

When you compare the Colani mouse, released in 1992 with the Microsoft mouse that came out in 1993, it is similar. Colani calls it a bio design, a biological design. It helps to differentiate us from others.

But design alone does not make people decide what product to buy. They want a technical product with certain features. If there are five similar products at the same price, with the same performance, then people will buy the Colani for the look. It is different. But they won't pay a lot more for the name. The challenge we face is to deliver the same or better performance, for the same or a lower price.

But otherwise I do not believe computer brands are very aspirational, as are watches such as Rolex or even perhaps cameras such as Nikon or Leica. With a technical product it is difficult, because technical products are judged by their technical features. Even a brand like Sony is only good if their products are good. They have the best picture tubes for TVs and computer monitors. But if their engineers fail, their marketing will fail also. This you can see from all Japanese companies. Toshiba is no longer the leader in the notebook business, which has nothing to do with the Japanese image or because they are very smart or whatever. It is the product, a scientific technical product, which has to stand up. On the other hand, watches are works of art, they are a statement. They are totally different. A watch is not thought of as a technical product.

THE TOOLS OF THE FUTURE

Over the next few years, I think the most important tool will still be the pen! As soon as there is a special task to do, such as in my own case, when I have discussions with suppliers to calculate prices on everything, I need a spreadsheet, a pen and a small calculator. I use the Hewlett Packard HP 95 LX, a very nice machine with built-in Lotus 1-2-3. I also have all my addresses and telephone numbers in it, so I don't have to change them every year when I start a new diary.

The personal digital assistant (PDA), such as Apple's Newton, holds some promise. But I don't like the idea of having to use a special pen (it does not have a keyboard, you write directly onto the screen and it converts this into characters). You lose the pen or leave it somewhere and where are you? Nothing is really happening yet in this area.

Say you have a personal computer or notebook and somebody tells you something about a sub notebook or a palmtop. People who have a desktop PC say, no, it's not enough. People who come from the other end, who are now using Casio or Sharp organisers find it too difficult to handle. So there is still some distance to go.

As for linking this to a cell phone, I think the cellular telephone network needs to be improved. Too often there is an interruption in the signal. I have a fax in my car, but I never use it anymore because as soon as it starts receiving, it gets a break and you end up with only two lines of text. Deutsche Telekom has announced the Modacom Network in Germany for data transmission from hand-held computers, but it will take some time for this to come in.

I think the Euro-executive of the next few years will have a desktop computer, a notebook at home and an organiser or PDA when out or travelling – three products. The computer will have a high-resolution 14 or 15-inch colour screen. It will have at least four megabytes (mb) of RAM, probably more. The new programs are more powerful and need a lot of RAM. The hard disk drive will be huge. The one we have been selling is 105 mb, now it's already up to 170 and by the end of 1993 it will be 250, by 1994 it will be 340 – by 1998 it will be one gigabyte (1000 mb) because it will cost the same as today's 170. Even the notebook of 1999 will have a 1 gb hard disc in it.

Both the desktop and notebooks will have fax modems, and probably the PDA, too. People can send either faxes or tap into their mainframe computer to get electronic mail (E-mail) or figures from their database.

As far as voice-control of computers is concerned, I have this vision of a room full of people controlling their computers by speech. One person says 'save' and the person at the next seat say 'erase'! What's the poor computer going to do?

The new capability of dropping a voice message into a document might be useful, if it's properly introduced, especially with E-mail. But I know one big company that installed an E-mail system costing half a million D-marks with all these functions. All that people are doing is exchanging recipes! So the problem is that not everything that is technically possible is necessarily useful.

Vobis structure

We made the decision in 1990 to sell 50 per cent of our company to Kaufhof Holding AG and they recently increased their share to 65 per cent. The remaining shares are split equally between myself and my co-founder, Rainer Fraling. This gave us much better cards to play. Kaufhof brought financial and management power. They operate Metro Cash and Carry and a chain of department stores.

23 per cent of our sales are made outside of Germany and 70 per cent of our foreign subsidiaries are very successful. We have some companies with difficulties, but that is normal in the first two years.

We will be expanding into the UK during 1993, but the basis has not been determined as yet. It has to happen. Maybe we'll open our own store, or do a joint venture, or maybe we will have dealers but we will be there in 1993.

We will be expanding later into Scandinavia, Greece, Portugal, Turkey and the Czech Republic. But when you have DM 2 billion total sales, to add a small country does not bring too much – maybe another two per cent. Perhaps we will do it by franchising – this is much faster than opening our own stores.

It is more important that even if there is a saturation of the market we still make money. To do this we must keep a very lean organisation. We have three managing directors, namely one CEO and two other members of the board, who deal with purchasing and marketing/product development. Staying so lean is the most difficult thing I ever did in my life. It may be impossible to do this, to keep the organisation as it was three or four years ago.

The question is, is it possible to run a company like air conditioning, so you can turn it down or up, or on and off? What can you do? I cannot do everything myself so I need people who will see what has to be done and do it. The challenge is to find those people who don't feel they have to ask over and over again: 'Is this right, is that wrong?' I need them to do it themselves. I have to change myself a little and let go. Being the founder is very difficult.

QUALITY

Vobis is certificated to ISO 9000 standards, which is very rare in Germany. In the UK many more companies have a quality accreditation, but in Germany only 1,000 have it, out of maybe 300,000 manufacturing companies. Quality is different from service and support because the better the quality is, the less support you need. A Japanese company says the production has to be good, not so much the service.

We have a technical hotline in each branch, and many more at our headquarters in Aachen to help our customers if they have problems. These are staffed by experts and not only help the customer but they also provide us with constant input so that we can continuously improve our products.

As we are expanding into serving major users, we have to

develop on-site service (which means we will go to the user's location to service their equipment). We do not now have on-site service, since normally it's not necessary for the retail customer. In Germany it's quite accepted, with a TV for example, to bring it to the shop to get it repaired. But to build our corporate business we need on-site service. This is something we must do.

IN REFLECTION . . .

My partner Rainer Fraling and I started in a garage (of course) when we were students at Aachen Technical University back in 1973. We began by selling pocket calculators to our fellow students. We opened up a mail-order business two years later as Vero GmbH. In 1981 we changed the name to Vobis, which is Latin for 'for you'. We opened our second branch in Düsseldorf in 1982 and began building our network of branches.

We concentrated on retailing computers, calculators and peripherals, but in 1984 we had a problem. We were selling various brands of computers, but we could not find a monitor at the right price. So we decided to build our own. Thus the Highscreen brand was born. We concentrated on making monitors for other people's computers. Then in 1987, once again, we had a problem. Right in the middle of the Christmas business period, two PC suppliers failed to make their delivery commitments. So we decided to build our own, and in 1988, the first 10,000 Highscreen PCs were sold. Five years later, we have just sold our 1 millionth Highscreen PC.

We got where we are through speed and flexibility. We keep it simple. We respond to our customers and give them precisely what they want. That is our strategy.

Theo Lieven, Chairman

Theo Lieven was born in 1952. He initially studied as a concert pianist and still plays (in fact he has recorded his first CD under the title *Vive les amateurs du piano*). He switched to the study of mathematics at Aachen Technical University and developed an interest in business.

Dropping out of school to concentrate on business, he started what has become Vobis with a partner in 1975. Today he is chairman of an organisation that turned over DM 1.5 billion in 1992.

In addition to playing the piano, Theo Lieven enjoys flying and spends some weekends teaching others to fly from a small grass airfield near his factory. He also flies his two company Cessnas, a Citation Jet and a Golden Eagle on business trips. He flew the Citation across the Atlantic on its delivery trip from the US.

He is a member of the wine fraternity Confrèrie des Chevaliers du Tastevin, and enjoys collecting old Leica cameras. He lives in Belgium: 'When I look out of the window I have to see at least five kilometres of greenery!'

Vobis Microcomputer AG, Aachen, Germany

Vobis Microcomputer AG was founded in 1975 by Theo Lieven and Rainer Fraling as Vero GmbH in Aachen, Germany. The name was changed to Vobis in 1981. In 1991 the company became a public limited company (AG) and is now owned 17.5 per cent each by Lieven and Fraling and 65 per cent by Kaufhof Holding AG.

Today, Vobis is Europe's top selling PC retail chain. Its business activities break down into two fields: distribution, with over 200 wholly-owned Vobis branches in 10 countries, and manufacturing (the Highscreen brand). Vobis currently has production centres in three locations in Germany and Austria. Combined maximum capacity is 4,300 PCs per day.

1992 turnover was DM 1.5 billion (up 53 per cent on 1991) with a workforce of 1,100. Foreign business accounted for 25 per cent of turnover. It is planned to raise the foreign turnover quota to 50 per cent in the medium term. Profits before tax rose to more than DM 60 million 1992 compared with DM 49 million in 1991.

With a total of 201 branches in 10 countries, Vobis is now Europe's biggest PC sales chain, with outlets in Germany, Austria, Switzerland, The Netherlands, Belgium, Italy, Spain, Luxembourg, Poland and France. All branches throughout Europe are designed along uniform lines, and the mainstay of their sales is the Highscreen PC, but other lines are offered as well.

4
Contract Catering

Catering for Europe

Garry Hawkes
Chief Executive,
Gardner Merchant Services Group

Contract catering will be one of the fastest growing service industries in Europe for the rest of the decade. But if the potential for feeding people is large, the opportunities for well-managed companies to become all-embracing facilities managers are vast.

Contracting out the catering facilities for employees of private or state organisations has really been a phenomena of the second half of this century. Certainly, it existed before – indeed the two companies that merged to form Gardner Merchant were founded in 1886 and 1928 – but it is only in the last 30 years or so that it has become big business.

But if growth has been rapid in recent years, there is still a lot to go for. Europe can be divided into three distinct development phases as regards contract catering. The business can be described as 'developed' in Belgium, France, Holland, Ireland, Italy and the UK; 'developing' in Germany and Spain; and 'embryonic' in eastern Europe.

'Developed' is, of course, only a relative expression and underplays the potential that exists even there. In the two most developed markets – France and the UK – independent contract caterers have only 38 per cent of the market. The current market size of the UK contract catering industry is £1.4 billion. The potential in the UK alone is over £3 billion.

Gardner Merchant is the largest catering company in Europe with about 14.6 per cent of the market. Our two nearest rivals are both French – Accor and Sodexho – with about 10 per cent and 9.5

per cent respectively, although Sodexho more closely resembles Gardner Merchant in its international outlook. Gardner Merchant dominates its home market with a 39 per cent market share, far outstripping its rivals.

INDUSTRY BACKGROUND

To appreciate the potential of the industry for companies and managers alike, it is helpful to take a brief look at how the industry has developed in the last 50 years.

Providing food for employees has several origins: paternalistic employers wanting to look after the workforce; enlightened self-interest in the belief that a well fed workforce is happier and works harder; control of habits and time – eating at the workplace cuts down the temptation to drink at lunchtime and shortens the time people need to take for lunch; and of course state enterprises that adopted the role of 'nanny'.

But until the aftermath of the Second World War, most organisations handled their catering in-house, having canteen staff on the direct payroll and dealing directly with food suppliers.

Providing a service is one thing. Providing a service that is both good and cost effective is quite another. Gradually a philosophy developed that organisations – be they banks, car manufacturers, armies, or scientific research establishments – were better off concentrating on their prime activity rather than trying to be all things to all men. From this developed the thought that necessary but ancillary services, such as catering, cleaning and security, were better contracted out to specialists. It made sense in terms of time management and efficiency. It made sense in terms of cost but above all, it made sense in terms of quality.

When it comes to food, quality and value are the most important of all. Employers might be able to get away with providing poor working facilities or out-of-date equipment. But provide poor, unappetising food and they soon know about it. If armies march on their stomachs, employees – from the shop floor to the company chairman – work from their stomachs. A grumbling stomach is a grumbling worker.

In war-ravaged Europe after 1945, the UK market developed the most quickly, mainly because its industrial infrastructure had been less damaged than elsewhere. There were cultural reasons as well.

But if France and Holland, for example, were relatively late starters, they quickly caught up with the UK. Germany has been much slower, but is now a very exciting market.

THE STATES OF CHANGE

The market changed in four significant aspects: (i) covering more organisations; (ii) providing catering services to all types of employees from the shop floor to the chairman; (iii) becoming large scale; and (iv) going international.

- **More Organisations**
  The provision of dining facilities expanded. It moved beyond just covering large scale industrial organisations employing thousands on one site: smaller companies and those in the white-collar areas, such as banking and insurance, moved to providing dining facilities.

- **More Employees**
  The market expanded to cover more and more employees. Where once there had just been works canteens – and often pretty grim ones at that – for manual workers, dining areas were increasingly provided for white-collar workers and then management itself.

  Gardner Merchant supplies food services to the board rooms of major corporations around the world. In the UK, we provide meals for the directors of companies such as ICI, Midland Bank and Hanson Trust; in Holland to KLM and ABN; in New York to the top lawyers at Skadden Arps. We also provide all the catering facilities to many of the North Sea off-shore oil platforms, schools, hospitals and old-people's homes. And at the other end of the scale, we even provide the catering in some of the prisons in Holland.

- **Growth of Scale**
  The third major change was one of scale. In the initial phase of the market development, much of the contracting-out was given to small sole operators who might have had one or two contracts. In the provision of food, particularly, big was once thought of as bad. There was a fear that large catering organisations would be impersonal, uncaring and providers of

standardised food. There was a fear that an organisation coming from another region in a country, or even another country, would try and impose alien food habits. In the early days, there were grounds for those fears. In fact, there still are, as the inexperienced, or just plain arrogant, try to impose their will instead of acknowledging cultural and culinary differences.

Recognising these differences, and listening to the requirements of our clients and their employees, has been one of the key elements to the success of Gardner Merchant. This attention to cultural nuances and regional differences cannot be overstressed: it is a corner stone of my philosophy. And it has been crucial in developing Gardner Merchant as Europe's largest caterer.

- **International Expansion**

    The fourth significant change in the market, was that it was able to develop internationally. In fact, international success can only come for those who can be successful on a national scale. Nations may seem homogeneous, but in fact they hide vast differences. The eating habits of those living in Manchester are completely different from those in London. Indeed, the culinary differences between Glasgow and Edinburgh in Scotland, which are only 30 miles apart, are significant. If you do not recognise those differences you have no hope of success. And if that is true for Scotland, imagine the differences between Amsterdam, Lyons and Birmingham.

    Of course, food has become much more international in the last half of the century as mass travel has opened up people's horizons and exposed them to different cultures and tastes. But that should not allow anyone to delude themselves that eating habits have become the same around the world. Enjoying different foods on holiday or on a night out is one thing, sampling different tastes on an everyday basis in a working environment is something completely different.

THE LEARNING PROCESS

Like any business, we, of course, have made our own mistakes, but they have been small and the lessons learnt from the experiences have been taken to heart. One mistake was the company's first foray into Germany back in 1973. Two major errors were made. First, too much emphasis was placed on language and not enough on management ability. The result was that we had Germans who could speak English and English people who could speak German, but they were not up to the management task. Secondly, not enough research had been carried out to see if the business environment was right. And it was not. But we learned quickly. Now we will go into a new country by buying a local operation and letting it keep its own identity and culture. We can graft onto that certain management tools to aid expansion, but it remains a local operation. You cannot force change in such a fundamental personal area as the provision of food. At best, you can act as a catalyst to change, but you cannot lead.

Our first successful move onto mainland Europe came in 1973 when we bought Van Hecke in Holland. We kept the local management and learned from them. I went over to Holland to help develop the market and oversee expansion into other parts of Europe. It worked and it is a model we have followed ever since.

When we went back to Germany a second time, we handled it from Holland and the move has been a great success.

GLOBAL OPPORTUNITIES

Gardner Merchant now operates around the globe – in Japan, the Far East, Australia, North America, and Europe. All the markets are expanding, but Europe is our backyard and, with all the vast cultural differences, is exacting and exciting.

The business potential is enormous. Harnessing that potential requires an effective management philosophy, not only in the abstract but in practice. For many, the potential will be but a chimera, ever unattainable, because they do not have the right perspective. It is not an industry for those who would rule by dictat or through strongly centralised and bureaucratic controls.

THE CHALLENGE OF DISPERSEMENT

Gardner Merchant already employs 46,000 people around the world, spread over 5,243 outlets. That is an average of less than 9 people per site, including allowances for the necessary headquarters and regional administrative staff. How do you offer consistent quality and standards in such a diffuse organisation?

BUSINESS PHILOSOPHY

Gardner Merchant may be a large company, but our thinking is dominated by 'small is beautiful'. It has to be, otherwise we would be trying to impose our views on our clients rather than being attuned to their needs and requirements.

And the key to that is empowerment of management and staff to do the job in the way they believe is right for their particular client. Power and with it responsibility is passed down to every level – and there are not many levels because an hierarchical structure is the antithesis of such a management attitude. Each of our 5,243 sites is its own profit centre.

Our staff are given ownership of their own units and projects. They take pride in their work because it is theirs and they get the glory both from the client and from the company when they do well. They are all individuals, not mere ciphers.

We believe in continuity of employment, both in a particular job and with the company. If people do a job well and enjoy it, we leave them where they are rather than moving them on for the sake of it. Clients and customers respond positively to continuity. That is why people like the Savoy Hotel in London so much: whenever you go back you see the same faces, someone who recognises you and greets you personally.

But we encourage people to maximise their talents, to extend themselves. If they do not succeed, there is no disgrace in failure, another job is sought for them. They go to another assignment. A company culture that punishes failure will never encourage people to stretch themselves and it will be just a mediocre company.

We believe in teamwork – and that goes for managers too, who are an integral part of the team. They should know everything about their operations, should be able to do every job. I believe in management by leadership, and that does not come from sitting behind a desk. For myself, I am out of the office at least three days a week, walking the job. I visit every country or region at least once a year so that I get first-hand experience of what is happening on the ground.

It is a cliché to talk about people businesses. But Gardner

Merchant is people. We have worldwide fixed assets of just £39 million, or less than £850 for each of our 46,000 employees. That is why 1,000 of our managers participated in the £402 million buy-out of the company earlier in 1993. It was not just a handful of the managers keeping all the action to themselves. And we are looking at ways of including all our staff in the ownership of the company.

Onto this well-spring of individuality we build a common, company-wide set of ethics, management philosophy and service standards that can work in harmony with the cultural and working practices found in our different markets. All our managers go through induction and refresher courses at our training establishment at Kenley, south of London, in order to establish this common culture.

As a company we invest heavily in training and technical development. We look on this in the same way that, say, a pharmaceutical company invests in research and development. R&D leading to new drug discoveries represents their future earnings. Our investment in the quality of our staff represents our future earnings.

It is development of our staff, allied with the policy of buying local operations and letting them have their head that assures me that we will be able to grasp the vast potential in Europe, never mind the rest of the world, as we head to the start of the new century.

HUGE SCOPE

As I mentioned, even the 'developed' catering markets in Europe have huge scope. This is aided by Governments and state organisations beginning to either privatise parts of the state machinery or open up state organisations to private enterprise and competition.

The initiative really started in the UK with Mrs Thatcher's governments. The concept of pulling back the state's boundaries is spreading throughout Europe in the search for efficiency and value for money. Even so we are still only scratching the surface.

In the UK, for example, National Health Service hospitals are being encouraged to seek value for money by contracting out their catering requirements, but less than five per cent have done so. Similarly, only just over 1 per cent of state primary and secondary schools have brought in contractors. Matters are somewhat more advanced in the police and fire services and at Ministry of Defence establishments, but there is still considerable scope for more business. That is the potential just in the UK.

Another burgeoning market is event catering. The number and frequency of large sporting, cultural and business events is increasing rapidly. And with it, the sophistication and demands of the public for good quality food also grows. That places an even greater demand on the abilities and flexibilities of caterers. Inevitably, the small scale operators are unable to cope with the extra requirements. For Gardner Merchant the opportunities are already there to win additional business as well as new ones that are constantly being created.

Event catering is an area we know very well. To give just a few examples in England, we handle all the catering at the Wimbledon Tennis Championships, as well as keeping all the spectators at the glittering Royal Ascot Week well supplied with food and champagne. We also provide all the catering for the Queen's large garden parties at Buckingham Palace.

THE PROMISE OF FACILITIES MANAGEMENT

Perhaps the biggest opportunity – and challenge as well – for organisations such as Gardner Merchant is in facilities management. Until now the provision of essential ancillary services such as cleaning, security, maintenance and even gardening at offices and factories have been handled by a plethora of suppliers, each sticking to its own area.

Increasingly large commercial and industrial companies are looking for economies of scale, efficiency and ease of administration in handling these requirements. Such contracts have many similarities to catering contracts and demand the same management and service ethos.

Becoming a full-service contractor by offering these additional services is a natural area of expansion for Gardner Merchant. Where we do not believe we have the necessary in-house skills either in a particular service or country, we will acquire people or businesses to give us the necessary base and then grow from there.

It is pleasing to be able to look to the future with excitement and in anticipation of tremendous business opportunities. The biggest threat to Gardner Merchant would be if we ever became complacent. After all we are by far the largest caterer in the UK and western Europe. We feed two million people around the world every day. But when it comes to their stomachs – be they the chairman of a major multinational or a shop floor worker – two million people are not going to let us get complacent.

Garry Hawkes

Garry Hawkes, aged 53, is Chief Executive of Gardner Merchant and has spent most of his working life with the company. He joined one of the predecessor companies, Peter Merchant, in 1963 as a District Supervisor and by 1972 was the UK North West Regional Director.

In 1976 he went to Holland to manage the new acquisition, Van Hecke, and to oversee the company's expansion into Europe. Two years later the Dutch expansion was such a success (Gardner Merchant's Dutch subsidiary is now the largest caterer in Holland and the country's 35th largest company) that Mr Hawkes was recalled to England to take over Gardner Merchant as Managing Director. He joined the main board of the then holding company, Trusthouse Forte, in 1986.

He masterminded a successful £402 million management buy-out, in which 1,000 managers invested, in January 1993.

Garry Hawkes is a strong proponent of management by partnership and empowering all staff at all levels of Gardner Merchant to take power and responsibility.

Gardner Merchant

Gardner Merchant employs 46,000 people worldwide. It is the UK and Europe's largest catering company. It also has expanding operations in Japan, China, Australia and the Far East, Africa, the Middle East, and North and South America. Annual turnover has doubled to £936 million in the five years to 1992.

The company was formed through a merger of the UK's then two largest contract catering companies – Peter Merchant and John Gardner – in 1966. It was wholly owned by hotel group Forte until January of 1993 when 1,000 managers and external investors bought it for £400 million.

Gardner Merchant is notable for the way it adapts itself to local cultures, which enables it to provide culinary services to peoples as diverse as the English, French, North Americans, the Japanese and the Arabs.

5
Courier Services
The Challenges Ahead in Courier Services

Robert M Kuijpers

Chief Executive Officer, Europe, Africa,
DHL Worldwide Express, Brussels, Belgium

I think you'll agree that the small package-delivery firm as typified by my company is coming of age – it's maturing. We've all been through a lot, attempting to put together the right combinations of networks, technology and service package, to serve the right combinations of customer. That was the pioneering stage.

Now we're well past the point of figuring out how to do what we do. We're into much more serious and sophisticated issues . . . like survival!

What is required to survive in this highly competitive market? We must recognise the real issues that we must be concerned with today, and do something about them. We are moving from being a supplier of only emergency services to being an important part of the planned logistics chains; this leads to new challenges! Here's my list of challenges:

- managing growth;
- regulatory issues;
- environmental issues;
- customs issues; and
- service improvements, or delivering what we promise.

Surrounding these is a constant need to maintain an entrepreneurial spirit as we continue to mature. We must stay close to our customers. We must recognise their needs as we address the questions and issues in our decision-making process.

MANAGING GROWTH

There's an increasing overlap between service providers – between forwarders and integrators; all kinds of different companies are moving in the same broad field. So there's an increasing need to differentiate between these services in responding to customer requirements.

Customers seem to realise that for logistical reasons they have demands for different types of service. For example:

- overnight/fastest possible delivery;
- time-definite service;
- heavy package categories and consolidations; and
- choice of pick-up/delivery locations.

I think the issue here is, does the customer want all possible services from one provider, or from several different providers, according to the providers' specialities and their own needs?

The players in the industry must make a choice. We can't be everything to everybody as we mature. We have to be honest and frank in our communications about what we can do for our customers.

How, then, can the customer differentiate between us all? Here are some of the advertising slogans of our industry:

- all you need to reach out (TNT);
- as sure as taking it there yourself (UPS);
- delivering the goods (Securicor);
- overnight success everyday (Elan);
- the power to deliver (Parcel Force);
- when it absolutely, positively has to be there on time (Federal Express);
- you know it's arrived the moment it's sent (DHL); and
- we keep your promises (DHL).

In view of the challenges we all face, we players can't be all things to all people. We have to carve out our own niches.

FUTURE TRENDS

How do we see the future of our market? At DHL we see an increasing market for people sending smaller packages on a regular basis.

There is a growing trend towards just-in-time delivery. This technique is being used more and more in manufacturing and distribution. As a concept, it has enabled the reduction of inventories, with a tremendously positive affect on profitability. Just-in-time delivery is what our industry is about.

The globalisation of resources, supported by the air express industry, is also having a very positive effect on manufacturers' profitability. Assembly of components from many different countries, all built to the same standards of quality, and once again delivered just in time, is enabling producers to build their offerings in the most cost-efficient way. They rely on air express for this capability in planned distribution.

We must be ever mindful of cost-effectiveness and profitability. It's all very well to develop great ideas, and to execute them with finesse. But a great idea is a not-so-great idea if it makes a negative contribution to the bottom line or creates an uneconomical return on investment.

DIVERSIFIED UPLIFT

In serving this market, we think the industry should use all types of transport, as appropriate. As a company with our own fleet of 55 aircraft, 70 operated charter aircraft, 8,285 courier vehicles, and 14 major hubs throughout the world, we still believe in using available external uplift capacity where it makes sense. We are an important customer for many major airlines. It's a question of managing resources effectively, and having standards to which we can hold our suppliers and partners.

As for resources, I include the potential of some of the military airports that are becoming available for recycling. The operators of several of these seem to think their future lies in serving the needs of the freight integrators only. But I think there is room for many users at these airports and with some exceptions, they should not restrict themselves to integrators.

With uplift, I include rail, if the capacity is there. But when using rail, it should not be according to the old Railway Administration rules. It should be according to the emerging needs of our customers. Old rules must change.

REGULATORY ISSUES

These involve governments in which officials will have to accept that our industry plays an important role to globalise trade and to make Europe work. Let's look at two regulatory issues that are facing the industry.

Postal Green Paper

The EC Green Paper for the postal industry is now with us. It refers to two sectors, the 'Reserved Sector', which is private mail with little or no added value, and which is traditionally a state monopoly and the 'Non-Reserved Sector', home of the value-added providers, such as ourselves, where competition should be fully open and untrammelled by unnecessary regulation. There should be no limitations in the value-added sector. The challenge ahead is to live in a world with a continuing reserved-sector service.

Freedom in the skies

The authorities should realise the importance of our industry for their national manufacturers, and that to operate effectively we need efficient line-haul opportunities and this requires us to have more freedom in the skies and on the roads than there is today. So-called fifth-freedom rights (allowing a foreign flag carrier to operate within or between other countries, for example British Airways carrying passengers from Paris to Nice) should be made available in Europe.

ENVIRONMENTAL ISSUES

The kinds of environmental issues we are involved in are noise, waste and atmospheric pollution.

Noise

People don't like to sleep in houses near airports that become hives of activity in the middle of the night, with dozens of aeroplanes coming and going. But if we who fly those planes can show that we are good neighbours, the actual benefits of hub proximity can be seen to vastly outweigh the imagined negatives.

Being a good neighbour means flying very quiet aircraft on flight paths designed to minimise noise intrusion to the community. This is increasingly the case, a trend which must continue.

Waste

As far as waste is concerned, we must continue to strive for improvements in packaging that is friendly to the environment. Do we really co-operate with the packaging industry to develop more environmentally friendly packaging? If we do not, then we should.

Emissions/run-offs

The latest engines used in our aircraft burn fuel very cleanly indeed. Emissions from our diesel trucks minimise air pollution. De-icing fluids used on our aircraft must find their way to an unharmful end after they have done their work.

We must constantly keep environmental impact high on our agenda as we specify new and replacement equipment and supplies.

CUSTOMS ISSUES

The single-European market can help our industry. And, of course, our industry can only help the single-European market achieve its promise. But companies moving packages in and out of the EC are still finding a lot of Customs formalities. Our industry has already taken a leading role in smoothing these out, but we have some way to go yet. It can still be true that a package spends longer in Customs than it does getting to its destination.

Let me reiterate the steps that we believe are necessary to improving the customs interface:

- bonded sorting facilities on the airports to enable faster transfers of materials;

- 24-hour dedicated Customs at key hubs, if necessary funded by our industry;
- streamlined dutiable valuations that provide the expected Customs revenue with minimum paperwork and individual assessments;
- pre-arrival Customs clearance to increase time available for this; and
- increased use of electronic data interchange, working from data that is input at the start of a shipment's life cycle rather than at different points in its journey.

What it boils down to is uniform and harmonised global protocols for Customs clearances. National Customs authorities must recognise the benefits of these and act to bring this dream closer to reality.

VALUE-ADDED TAX

The complexities of VAT will not go away. We now see the end of zero-rating for VAT on cross-border shipments within the EC, adding to complexity for intra- and extra-Community shipments. And what about billing in a third country? As governments still require statistical information, so reporting of shipment information will be required, involving different treatment of data. Some of our customers will look to us to provide these data. This will lead to an increase in our costs and therefore lead to increased costs for our customers, which is the total opposite of the goals in Europe after 1993.

SERVICE IMPROVEMENTS

Just because we've come up with a solution to a customer need, developed it and launched it doesn't mean we are allowed to stop there. We have to keep refining the result, in the light of experience in the real world. If we do it right, we can keep going for ages. But once more, we need the support of the regulatory bodies to improve our offering.

No matter how brilliant our solution, and how many changes we engineered before it was finally launched, when it does appear in the marketplace, it could still stand improvement. If we don't make the improvements, someone else will.

Think of some of the innovative products or services that have been introduced in the last 20 years or so that have been superseded by a superior competitive idea: Betamax videotape vs VHS; stereo-8 tape cartridges vs compact cassettes; super-8 movie film vs videotape; and quadraphonic hi-fi sound vs CD. The challenge of continual upgrading and improving is also there for us in our industry.

CUSTOMER EXPECTATIONS

Customers always lead us. As Timothy Foster, the editor, said in his book, *101 Ways to Generate Great Ideas*:

> Innovators produce exciting solutions, sometimes so far ahead of expectations that minds are collectively blown – for a few moments. For no sooner has the solution arrived, than consumer expectations move ahead. So innovators address these new expectations, and, with luck, exceed them. The consumer looks at the result and says 'That's nice. But wouldn't it be nicer if it did this, as well?' They are never satisfied.

So it is our job to stay ahead of them.

Look at the technology of track and trace – following a package through its entire handling cycle with the service provider. We've come a long way, but we're not there yet. Instead of simply providing the shipper and receiver with real-time information about the whereabouts of their package, what do we have to do to make this process even more proactive?

For example, suppose there was a sudden air traffic control strike at Madrid – a pure fantasy, of course. What do we have to do to provide an early warning to the shipper or receiver that this could impact their delivery?

More important, what do we have to do to take account of this and provide an alternative solution that delivers a seamless result to the customer? An ATC strike in Madrid is not the customer's problem, it is our problem. What kind of signals do we need to send, and to whom, to facilitate an uncorrupted delivery?

This is a big challenge, and when you fold in the desire to be able to do this door-to-door on a worldwide basis, it can be seen that we have some distance to go.

Our pricing must reflect the need to recover the full cost of the huge investment we have made, and must continue to make.

TAKING ADVANTAGE OF THE NEW FREEDOM TO MOVE GOODS QUICKLY

Customer service in many industries can be improved so that 98 per cent of orders are filled the first time from existing supplies, while at the same time, inventories can be cut in half. This is the promise of *our* industry. With the increasing popularity of just-in-time delivery, warehousing needs are being reduced by companies with the sophisticated systems necessary to help them stay on top of what is needed, where and when.

This reduction in space, inventory and staffing is having a significant positive impact on the bottom line. But 'just-in-time' is just the first step in the chain of improved efficiency. The next step is the global optimisation of manufacturing and distribution activities. This means global specifications, global standards, and the global harmonisation of systems. It means taking advantage of our global promise. Companies at the forefront of these distribution techniques are our best customers.

THE FUTURE

We've seen air express doubling every three years because it is growing with the way business is changing. It is serving new businesses, in new marketplaces, as both grow bigger together. It is here to stay. We have the technology to support the rapid movement of goods. There is a constant move towards global trade liberalisation. Rising customer expectations are increasing the need for better service, using new distribution techniques.

Together, these factors are creating a unique opportunity we must not miss. Our industry will help provide the rapid circulation needed in the new marketplaces:

- Europe, West and East;
- North America; and
- Asia-Pacific.

We have to work together, all of us, the air-express industry, the airlines, the airports, governments and businesses, to help remove the last constraints to global trade and fulfil the promise for the future we know exists. We should lead this process, which is essential to global economies.

Robert M Kuijpers

Robert Kuijpers joined DHL in 1988 as CEO for Europe and Africa, moving there from his role as Managing Director for Central Europe with H J Heinz Europe. In addition to managing the DHL group activities in Europe and Africa, Mr Kuijpers is responsible for DHL subsidiary companies such as European Air Transport, the wholly-owned DHL airline; ELAN, the ground transport company; and the DHL European Sorting Centre at Brussels National Airport.

He had previously held top marketing and sales positions in Western Europe at Aspro Nicholas, Sterling Products and Beecham before he joined H J Heinz in 1972.

He is a former Dutch tennis international and is still active in the sport.

DHL Worldwide Express

Founded in the US in 1969, DHL is the pioneer of the door-to-door air express industry. The company currently employs some 28,000 people in more than 215 countries serving more than 80,000 destinations.

DHL Worldwide Express is composed of DHL International Ltd, which serves all locations outside the US and its territories and DHL Airways, Inc., which serves all locations within the US and its territories. DHL's International Worldwide Coordination Centre is in Brussels as is the regional headquarters of Europe and Africa.

6
Foods

Managing Change in Manufacturing Organisations

Edward S Moerk
President,
Campbell Biscuits Europe, Brussels

The European food industry will see more change over the next 10 years than in the last 40, because of three developments taking place at the same time: first, the restructuring of Europe's industry and the consolidating of competitive positions in every area of the food chain. Second, the replacement of the traditional forms of organisation and management for European operations by new organisational concepts such as networking organisations. And third, for lack of a better word, the 'Americanising' of European food and consumption habits, eg, nearly everyone goes to McDonald's, nearly everyone eats corn flakes and so on.

I believe that dramatic change requires dramatic response. European food manufacturers must challenge the classical myth: that local food habits and taste buds are too diverse for a pan-European business approach to be effective. Food companies need to restructure both their organisations and their thinking. This is what we have done over the last two years at Campbell Biscuits Europe.

CREATING AND MANAGING CHANGE AT CAMPBELL'S

In 1989, our company was on the divestment list of Campbell Soup, with profitability, investment and innovation on the downswing for years. Here was a middle-sized, multinational, $280-million-in-sales company with no European focus, five complete country-based operations, eight plants, five different brand names, 100 different products, three different logos, five advertising agencies and conservative managers whose main purpose was to preserve their local country 'kingdoms'. Costs were out of control and the numbers miserable – the company was losing millions of dollars because of an Italian subsidiary, Lazzaroni. This was the situation as I took charge.

Within 60 days, we developed a three-phased game plan which was:

1. stop the losses and save the company;
2. dramatically upgrade financial and organisational performance; and
3. implement growth and investment initiatives to make Campbell Biscuits Europe an attractive part of Campbell's future.

Now, two years later, we are in phase three and on track for an exciting future. What did we do?

We developed our vision for our industry

We believe there will be major rationalisations in the biscuit industry over the next 10 years. The number of plants will decrease from 600 to 150, the industry will increasingly go from hand-crafting to mass production and mass marketing and we will see an industry traditionally dominated by one to three national players in each country, moving pan-Europe to establish pan-European competitive positions. The size of the leading companies will increase as some pursue production-driven strategies such as United Biscuits out of the UK, some a brand-driven strategy such as Bahlsen in Germany or ourselves, some a mixture. In 10 years there will be only three major, pan-European biscuit brands. Our brand, Delacre, will be one of them.

We developed a vision for Delacre

Delacre's vision is to be Europe's number one pan-European premium biscuit brand with strong positions in continental Europe and global exports. We position Delacre as French with products based on the best of traditional and new French *savoir–faire*, produced in a few state-of-the-art manufacturing plants in Europe, backed by a uniquely pan-European, lean organisation with state-of-the-art information and central-support systems.

This vision implies increased competition. We need to be a low-cost producer with high profitability. So we had to look at our cost structure and sources of profit. We sold the money-losing Italian Lazzaroni biscuit operations with two plants, which immediately, cut our bleeding. We reduced overheads by 15 per cent and eliminated a number of senior management positions.

We centralised production and sourcing

One person is now directly responsible for all of our plants, central purchasing and logistics. We took the plants away from the country manager, because 40 per cent of our production, including our popular *Assortments* range, goes on for further processing in another plant. We made further savings and halved our supplier base by consolidating quantities and developing a preferred-supplier system.

Country managers were not flattered by the removal of their responsibility for production. Some left, others accepted different responsibilities.

We developed a pan-European marketing strategy

This is the most controversial area of a pan-European restructuring because it challenges our basic belief of cultural, historical and food diversity between countries. We developed a pan-European positioning for Delacre as Europe's number-one premium biscuit and then employed a pan-European brand, packaging, agency and advertising approach.

- **One brand**
  This involved consolidating five local brands into one. We chose Delacre because of its pan-European and global potential and its strong premium connotation. Why one brand? Simple. You can't afford to dilute resources among five brands in the new pan-European game.

- **New packaging**
  We then developed a pan-European-umbrella packaging for Delacre consolidating 12 different packaging types and three

different logos into one pan-European design for 100 products sold in 50 countries. Interestingly, we used a leading Italian design company and an internal pan-European task force. The job was done in three months. By comparison it had taken the company two years to change one product in the past.

- **One ad agency, one PR agency**
  We believe in the advertising agency as an integral part of our European team. We moved on to consolidate six country-based local advertising agencies into one pan-European group, Ogilvy & Mather. O&M provides strong central leadership out of Paris for all countries where we are currently doing business or plan to. In the same spirit we appointed a pan-European PR and communications agency, Burson-Marsteller, with head-office in Brussels and we work with both agencies as pan-European teams.

- **Pan-European advertising**
  Advertising, to be utilised in all our national markets, positions Delacre in the pan-European context, but as a premium biscuit brand based on French *savoir-faire* and the finest biscuit know-how and ingredients. It establishes a brand platform for the next 10 years.

  Today we have the same campaign on the air in France, Belgium, Holland and Germany and on pan-European television networks CNN and MTV. In fact, Delacre was the first food brand in Europe to advertise on pan-European television. The campaign won the 1992 Cannes Gold Lion international advertising award for best commercial in the worldwide food and drink category. And it's in English – reaching 22 countries in Europe! Most important, the advertising works. Our tracking studies show brand attributes and awareness up in all countries and Delacre positioned as the French premium biscuit brand across these markets and recently the campaign was voted by consumers as number two out of 120 pan-European commercials in persuasion and preference.

- **Centralised new products strategy**
  We decided on strong centralisation of our new-products strategy and development and that we would focus 80 per cent of our resources into pan-European projects. One concrete example was the biscuit industry's first pan-European new

product launch for our *Biscuits Maison*, an adaptation of a Pepperidge Farm brand, in four locations simultaneously.

PAN-EUROPEAN NETWORK ORGANISATION

The traditional way of organising in the food industry is out of date. A new concept is required to match European opportunities with local executional needs, different nationalities, different interests, different food trade structures. I call this the integrated pan-European network organisation.

This is an organisation which has a strong centre, with leadership of strategic areas rather than a centre in the traditional bureaucratic sense of the European company. This network is based on shared values and purpose throughout the organisation with clear management accountabilities. It is an organisation focused on pan-European similarities and opportunities as opposed to differences, and requires a European as opposed to a country focus. It utilises resources wherever they are available in the organisation in a pragmatic way rather than following some pre-established bureaucratic process based on branches.

It is a concept of organisation we're in the process of developing. It is not easy, because it requires a clear sense of mission for the total European company; for everybody from the top to the shop floor, with a high degree of personal leadership and communication. It is much more difficult to lead and manage than the traditional hierarchical organisations which had clear 'command' approaches focused on a stable environment.

THE RESULTS

Profit over the two years following the start of this new strategy in Campbell Biscuits Europe was up 52 per cent. The company has moved from divestment to investment mode and changed from a production-driven to a truly pan-European marketing-driven organisation, closing a 100-year old plant in Vilvoorde and preparing major new capital investment projects. We have successfully challenged a number of traditional assumptions as to what can and cannot be done in the food industry and we have the organisation and the momentum to go forward in an exciting way.

By any standard, the pan-European restructuring has been a successful strategy for change to get ready for the future.

LESSONS LEARNED

So what are some of the lessons we can draw from our experience? Restructuring can be very effective as a major-change strategy, but there are a couple of things to keep in mind. First, it needs to be dramatic, decisive and fast. It should be one big change not many small ones.

Second, restructuring is most effective if it is done by a new leader within a very short time of taking charge. A research study by Insead showed that all successful leaders made major changes within the first 100 days of taking charge. Any organisation will accept change if it is done quickly, during the honeymoon period, when the newcomer's vision is fresh.

As far as a pan-European restructuring is concerned, our experience has been that the biggest resistance to change will come from the country organisations losing power. The real issue is not whether France is different from Germany, but which organisation has to give up power.

Everyone has a vested interest in the *status quo*. Be prepared to break the patterns of the past and look to the future. I talked to people in other countries and different industries to get fresh inputs. And last, be prepared to go 80/20, ie you're not going to be 100 per cent right with a major restructuring so you might as well accept that 20 per cent will be wrong and stay happy in the knowledge that some of the changes you made will have to be fine-tuned later.

Edward S Moerk

Edward S Moerk joined the Campbell Soup Company in November 1989 as President of Campbell's Biscuits Delacre, responsible for the company's European biscuit business with operations in France, Belgium, Germany and Holland as well as worldwide exports. In October 1992 he was named an officer of the Campbell Soup Company.

Before coming to Campbell, Mr Moerk was President of Canada Dry Corporation, USA, a division of Cadbury Schweppes Inc., based in Stamford Connecticut, from 1986 to 1989. From 1981 to 1986, he held various positions with PepsiCo Inc., including President Pepsi-Cola Brazil, based in Rio de Janeiro, Vice President Marketing of Pepsi-Cola Mexico and Director of Marketing Far East/China, Australia, based in Singapore.

He started his career with CPC International Inc., and had numerous marketing and new product assignments in Brussels, Amsterdam and the USA at CPC's Best Foods division. Mr Moerk grew up in Norway, studied in the UK and received an MBA from Insead, Fontainebleau in France.

Campbell Biscuits Europe

Campbell Biscuits Europe is part of the Campbell Soup Company, an American-based multinational with turnover of about $6.5 billion and 45,000 employees, known for such brands as Campbell Soup, Swanson Dinners, V8 juices, Pepperidge Farm, Delacre, Godiva Chocolates and D&L sauces.

In 1990, the Campbell Soup Company, under the leadership of new CEO, David Johnson, started a major restructuring to refocus the portfolio worldwide and position the company for profitable growth through core businesses: soups, sauces and biscuits. The financial results have been spectacular: two years of record profits and an increase in the company's stock price of nearly 70 per cent.

Campbell Biscuits Europe is part of Campbell's Worldwide Biscuit & Bakery Division, which, with sales of about $1.3 billion, ranks as the fourth large biscuit company in the world. The division consists of Delacre in Europe, Pepperidge Farm in the US and an interest in Arnotts, Australia's leading biscuit business.

In Europe, Delacre manufactures over 100 premium biscuit products which are marketed in over 50 countries mostly on the European continent. Delacre was started in fact by a Belgian 110 years ago. The company was bought by Campbell in 1962 and over time grew via export and small acquisitions.

7
Hotels and Restaurants
Developing an International Network of Branded Hotels and Restaurants

Rocco Forte
Chairman,
Forte PLC

Forte has grown in almost 60 years from a caterer with one restaurant into one of the world's largest owners and operators of hotels and restaurants. As we entered the 1990s we took the opportunity to analyse where we were and where we wanted to be. We had grown by acquisition and organically and had developed a wide range of products in what was a fairly unstructured industry. Now, in the words of our sign off, we say we are 'host to the world'. What are we doing about delivering on this promise?

Strategic review

We looked at our strengths and weaknesses and the opportunities and threats presented to us. We examined the potential of each business. We decided that if we wanted to keep pace with the biggest, in an industry which is consolidating into a small number of large global players, we had to concentrate our focus. We concluded we could not realistically aspire to be a world leader in all three of our core businesses – hotels, restaurants and contract catering.

Narrower focus needed

Thus we resolved to narrow our interests from these three businesses to two: hotels and restaurants. These were by far the largest of our operations, they employ similar skills and they largely serve the same customer base.

In spite of the good growth opportunities it presented, we decided to sell Gardner Merchant, our main contract catering organisation, to tighten our focus and free up cash for the rest of our businesses. We had built this company over the years and felt a strong loyalty to its people and its customers. We also knew we had to sell it in a way which kept the management and the customer base intact if we were to maximise shareholder value. So, at the start of 1993, it became the subject of a buyout by a group of institutions, with existing management taking a share. We retained a 25 per cent interest in the company.

WINNING CHARACTERISTICS

We had asked ourselves: What will be the characteristics of the successful hotel and restaurant business in the year 2000? We concluded that the growth we wanted would best come from branded operations served by an international sales, reservations and distribution system. Seasoned business travellers seek the security and dependability of a trustworthy brand. And the more inexperienced travellers rely on a well-known brand to help them deal with their relative lack of familiarity and confidence. Both wish to be able to make bookings anywhere in the world easily and quickly.

We determined that our future lay in businesses that would be large enough to justify the use of mass-media advertising and promotion, that would deliver economies of scale. We decided we would operate only businesses which were already market leaders or could be developed as such.

Thus in 1991 we reorganised the hotel division into brands or collections: Forte Travelodge, Forte Posthouse, Forte Crest, Forte Heritage, Forte Grand and Exclusive Hotels of the World. The restaurant division was already well structured in this way, incorporating brands such as Little Chef, Happy Eater, Harvester and Welcome Break, and we resolved to concentrate our resources on the main brands.

EXPANSION BEYOND THE UK

As market leader in the UK, we have a strong position. There is still some growth to come in the UK from better use of our existing hotels portfolio and growth of our main restaurant brands. But these alone will not meet our ambitions for the future. If we are to be one of the global players in the next century, and in the process reduce our dependence on the UK economy, international expansion must be clearly on our agenda.

The hotel business is very fragmented on this side of the Atlantic. In North America, 60 per cent of hotel rooms are within multiple operations, while in the UK the figure is 25 per cent. France is similar, but in other parts of Europe the proportions are much lower. In Italy, for example, only three per cent of rooms are owned by multiples.

The unstructured nature of these markets presents an opportunity in its own right. However, the fact that, as yet, there is no genuine pan-European hotelier makes the prize even greater. We believe there is a strong opportunity for our hotels in this area and that we can grow our roadside operations into Europe alongside our hotel development.

CONTINENTAL EUROPE

So continental Europe will indeed be a priority for Forte over the next decade, and we expect it to provide major growth despite the temporary current decline, reflecting the slowing economies in this area. Industry analysts agree that a fundamental driver of this growth will be the steady transition of these countries' economies from manufacturing to service industries. This transition accelerates business demand for hotels and as the economic structure changes, so the domestic leisure demand for hotels will grow strongly.

We have been growing on mainland Europe since we first acquired the George V and two other luxury hotels in Paris in 1965. We already have a hotel presence in most countries and a good network of sales offices. So we have experience and a good track record, but lack critical mass.

We took two important steps in this direction in early 1993. We acquired the Relais motorway restaurants group in France, which makes us the second largest player in that market and started a joint hotel venture with AGIP in Italy, which also gives us a very strong market position.

EASTERN AND CENTRAL EUROPE

I see three scenarios in this region. In the short-term there will be a need for quality hotels serving an international clientele in cities such as Warsaw, Prague and Moscow. In the medium-term, there could well be scope for budget properties to address domestic needs in many other cities. And in the long-term, say over the next 10 to 20 years, there could be a complete infrastructure build up as the regional economies mature and start to demand such things as roadside restaurants.

We will move cautiously in this area, in order to understand the environment, but we now have a proud presence in Warsaw, where in December 1992 we reopened the 5-star Hotel Bristol in a joint venture between Forte and Orbis, the Polish state tourist agency. We have since added to this with a Forte AGIP hotel in Budapest.

TURNING STRATEGY INTO ACTION

Fulfilling our strategy in these recessionary times means we must first concentrate on three principal areas:

- ensuring our products lead the increasingly competitive markets in which we operate;
- winning market share by enhancing our sales and marketing activities; and
- improving margins by reducing costs.

We are making progress. Despite falling demand in 1992 we maintained sales at the previous year's levels while improving trading profit considerably.

We have reorganised and reinforced our sales team, and we are developing a second-generation reservation system which will not only give us enhanced reservations capacity but also an improved customer information base and yield management capability.

We have increased our promotional spend and rebranded our hotels, as called for in our strategic review. This has provided us with a competitive edge. The resultant clearer definition of our products has made it easier to communicate our strengths to the customer, while the collective strength of the Forte name allows us to underline the size of our network and the choice we offer.

In the area of cost reduction, we have eliminated layers of management to bring decision makers closer to the customer. We have simplified our administrative structures and we have regionalised our support services to reduce administrative costs at individual hotels and restaurants.

We now employ a much more flexible workforce, both in terms of hours worked and multiskilling. This enables us to match our staffing levels to changes in demand at our hotels and restaurants, and gives much greater access to the variety of skills available in the local market.

Customer focus

Our new management structure has also seen us strengthen brand management by promotions from within and recruitment of key figures from the industry. This provides the opportunity for our people to get their arms around the business and pay attention to the detail that separates excellence from mediocrity. No matter how clever your strategy or your marketing, if you don't deliver at or above expectations in our business, you lose a customer at the end of the day. We have enhanced the quality of our product and the delivery of our service by concentrating on our customer's needs.

Guiding principles

The principles which have guided us in making our changes have been:

- one company with strong leadership and benefits of scale;
- clear focus on individual markets;
- strong management teams running brands;
- small, well-informed corporate team;
- entrepreneurial approach; and
- clear accountabilities with performance-related awards.

THE BUSINESS TRAVELLER OF THE FUTURE

I think there will be two sorts of business traveller in 2001. One will be very clearly price-driven. The other, the regular traveller who is on the road nearly every week, seeks variety and local culture. We serve both markets.

Businesses have become increasingly aware of the size of their spend on travel and entertainment and in the recent recessionary times companies have become more conscious of the need to curb such expenses. But they also recognise that travel and entertainment is essential to their business. People still need to meet people and negotiate one on one. This has led to many large companies negotiating their travel needs one on one, saying in effect: 'We will give you all our hotel business. Now what's your best rate?' Only the largest players can respond to these approaches and we are already seeing the benefits.

The hotel of the future will still be judged by the same key factors as the hotel of today: personal service, attention to detail, good food, pleasant rooms and value for money. It will no doubt have enhanced technology, but this will free up the staff so that service can become even more personalised, enabling us to deliver beyond the standards expected rather than to depersonalise the operation. If a guest in one of our hotels in London is in need of a reservation tomorrow in Milan, he or she can already book direct through our systems. I can see how it will eventually be possible to review details of the proposed hotel on the in-room TV, to view various aspects and different rooms, perhaps even see a short information briefing on the destination – all interactively under control of the guest.

Many of our rooms already have in-room fax machines and plugs for computer modems and are provided with video players. We shall obviously stay abreast of these technologies as they advance, always providing our guests with what they need when they're on a trip.

Video conferencing will increase. I do not see this as a threat since people will always want to meet face to face, but as an opportunity to become the logical venue for providing these facilities to those who want the service but do not wish to tie up their capital in expensive equipment.

THE IMPORTANCE OF TRAVEL AND TOURISM

Whatever the characteristics of the traveller of the future, and the makeup of the industry which serves them, there can be no doubt of the importance of our sector. According to the World Travel and Tourism Council, this is the world's largest industry, accounting for more than 6 per cent of GDP, 1 out of every 15 workers, 7 per cent of capital investment and 13 per cent of consumer spending worldwide.

The Council's research suggests that our industry's contribution to global GDP could double by 2005, that capital investment could increase by 80 per cent and that resultant employment could rise by 33 per cent, representing 40 million new jobs.

This growth depends on governments reflecting travel and tourism's role in mainstream economic policies to liberalise markets, improve infrastructure, reduce bureaucratic regulation, eliminate barriers to travel and diminish taxes on travellers and travel companies. If they take up this call, travel and tourism can and will provide the immediate economic stimulus and long-term growth prospects that all governments are seeking. Forte intends to be part of that growth into the next century and beyond.

Rocco Forte

Rocco Forte is the only son of Lord Forte, the founder of the Group. He was born in Bournemouth in 1945 and was educated at Downside School and Pembroke College, Oxford, where he read Modern Languages (French and Italian), gaining an MA. He went on to study accountancy and is a Fellow of the Institute of Chartered Accountants (FCA).

After several management positions within Forte, he was appointed to the board as Director of Personnel in 1973. He became Deputy Chief Executive in 1978 and Chief Executive in 1983. He took over the role of Chairman from his father in 1992.

He is a Director of the British Tourist Authority and a past President of the Hotel and Catering Benevolent Association. He is President of the British Hospitality Association and a Director of Savoy PLC. He lists his interests as running (he has completed several marathons), golf, shooting and fishing. He is married, with a son and two daughters.

Forte Plc

Charles Forte (now Lord Forte) opened the Meadow Milk Bar in London in 1935.

Now Forte is one of the world's leading hotel and catering companies. It is the UK market leader and has a significant presence throughout Europe and North America. In 1993, Forte Plc:

- employs over 47,000 people;
- has over 2,000 locations;
- operates in 37 countries; and
- serves about 200 million customers annually.

There are over 1,000 Forte restaurants with brands spanning the UK market such as Little Chef, Happy Eater, Harvester and Welcome Break to London's famous Cafe Royal. The roadside brands have recently moved into mainland Europe with operations in Germany, France and Ireland.

There are over 800 Forte hotels in over 30 countries. With 345 properties in the UK, Forte is by far the largest hotelier in the country. A further 64 properties are located elsewhere in Europe, the Middle East and the Caribbean. There also 450 hotels in North America.

Forte hotels are structured into brands and collections, each targeted on specific markets and offering clearly defined standards of service. These brands cover a range from budget accommodation to some of the world's best luxury hotels, including London's Grosvenor House, the Plaza Athenee and George V in Paris, the Hotel des Bergues in Geneva, The Excelsior Hotel Gallia in Milan, the Ritz in Madrid, the Bristol in Warsaw, the Dom in Cologne as well as the Westbury in New York, the Watergate in Washington, and the King Edward in Toronto.

Fiscal 1993 sales were £1.9 billion and gross profits were £297 million.

8
Information Technology

Trends in the European Information Technology Services Market

Vernon Ellis

*Managing Partner, Europe,
Andersen Consulting, London*

INTRODUCTION

Are we in Europe delivering maximum value in information technology (IT) to end users? The answer, I'm afraid, is that we are not.

For users and customers all over Europe, the bloom seems to have faded from the rose of information technology. They remember all the great things IT was supposed to deliver and they see also how performance seems to have failed to match the promise.

But is their perception correct? And, if so, how has it come to this? Let's consider the whole question of IT from the perspective of value.

CHANGING VALUES IN IT

Value is to a large extent in the eye of the beholder, or more relevant to consultants like us, the customer. And expectations are changing.

Yesterday, information technology was all about making it happen. Originally speed, power and processing capacity were at a premium. The value of information technology was often measured in terms of quantity of input MIPS, size of systems departments, and so on. Or we could measure output – lines of code, for example.

Of course, we have learnt that there has to be more to it than just delivering the technology. First there are the fundamentals of testing, project management and training. Then the wider aspects of systems integration. That is how service providers have built their businesses.

But the ground rules keep shifting. What we once thought were sources of value are today mere commodities. Today, it is not the technology, it is what we do with it. The issue is to deliver value to the business in terms of improving the performance of the customers we serve – performance in terms of effectiveness, customer service and market share.

THE DRIVERS OF CHANGE

This performance improvement is absolutely vital to nearly all our customers. We live in an era of unparalleled and accelerated change:

- change driven by global competitiveness;
- change driven by new customer demands;
- change driven by technology.

To dominate or just survive requires continuous change. I need not rehearse the drivers for change in more detail, they are well known, but it is worth dwelling on a couple of features specific to Europe.

The changes arising from production and trade integration will continue to intensify, Maastricht or not. The real steps have already been achieved: lowered trade barriers and the harmonisation of standards. So regardless of what happens on the political stage, the sheer relentless cost pressures to rationalise in Europe will see that it happens.

The second feature of note in Europe is the wave of commercialisation and privatisation which is beginning to roll across the continent. The UK has been in the vanguard of this change and we have worked with many of the major utilities in totally transforming the way they deliver service to the customer. Even governments are beginning to reorient their processes around the needs of the citizen.

Everywhere we look, change is non-optional. The survival and success of many organisations depends on enabling, achieving and sustaining change. But change is not easy; successful change is harder still. It requires the right frame of mind, the focus on the long-term aim, the consistency of purpose.

DIFFERENT ATTITUDES TO CHANGE

Do these attitudes flourish in European business? Consider the five words most frequently used by these players:

- Success;
- Profit;
- Growth;
- Target; and
- Result.

These are all desired ends. But they give no recognition to the process to get there or stay there.

Compare those with the business culture of Japan, as portrayed by their five most frequently used words:

- *Doryuku* – effort;
- *Nintai* – perseverance;
- *Arigato* – thank you;
- *Seijitsu* – loyalty; and
- *Kanjo* – tenacity.

The Japanese have core attitudes which balance the will to win with the freedom to fail – which means they not only strive for continuous improvement (*kaizen*) but also tend to learn and profit from their mistakes. The importance of teams encourages implementation of change by consensus and the sharing of information.

There are signs that Japanese attitudes and values may be migrating west. Just-in-time principles applied right across the logistics chain are becoming better understood. The concept of partnering – the creation of a true win/win relationship rather than a win/lose relationship – is also coming to the fore amongst enlightened companies. Above all, there seems to be a greater realisation that structural change is necessary.

From anecdotes and literature one might think that the Americans are streets ahead of Europe in realising the need for this structural change. After all, 'restructuring' and 're-engineering' are hot issues in the USA. This may just be due to higher speed of dissemination – more business magazines recycling the same examples. Also the cynics will say that it is a passing fad (the Americans do tend to be more faddish than the Europeans).

But then what is a fad? And how do you distinguish it from genuine interest and innovation? It could be very dangerous for us here in Europe to dismiss American enthusiasm for business re-engineering as just the latest buzzword.

THE ROLE OF IT IN FACILITATING CHANGE

What role can IT play in this wholesale restructuring? Potentially, an important one. An article written by Rudy Puryear of Andersen Consulting and Peter Keen, business guru and author, argues that business networking removes traditional barriers of time and location. There is particular potential for that here, for Europe.

Liberation from traditional time and distance barriers provides companies in Europe with a real opportunity to exploit the full potential of the single market – before their competitors do. Take, for example, logistics, which has become, almost overnight a board-level concern. The reason for this is simple. In most industries Europe has far too many plants compared to, say, the USA. It is easy to see how costs could be saved by rationalising production across Europe. But logistics immediately becomes enormously more complex.

This is only the start. Re-thinking distribution is not just a matter of warehousing, inventory and transportation. It has to tackle other related areas such as urban crowding and recycling. The organisational and change-management challenges which flow from this are quite daunting and most multinationals trying to reconfigure their operations across Europe are struggling with these issues.

Here are two other examples where technology's change is only half the story: in retail banking, the customer focus has been lost. This is partly a matter of information. Banks are bogged down in

1970's technology with non-integrated account systems. It also is a question of culture and the attitude of branch personnel. Another example: hospitals are extraordinarily inefficient. Doctors and nurses travel amazing distances in their daily rounds. We measured seven miles as the average distance travelled by junior doctors in a recent study. Even patients are pushed around on long journeys. Enormous improvements can be brought about by patient-centred reconfiguration. The technology to support this is available. But the resistance to change is considerable – at all levels.

THE INTEGRATED APPROACH

At the heart of these re-engineering changes lies the enabling mechanism of information and information technology – not IT alone. Trying to exploit information technology independently – without looking at the other elements of the business process and even more important, the people involved – is a recipe for discord and disharmony.

It is also counter-productive, for what you are really doing is automating the *status quo*. Or, as a business strategy director of Xerox in Europe put it: 'We have embedded our sub-optimal processes in silicon'.

The depth of changes envisaged in these three examples can only be brought about by a much more comprehensive approach, a fusion of *strategy processes* and *people technology*.

A useful analogy for the change process is to think of the three elements: people, processes and technology, as three playing pieces on a peg board, trying to advance towards their end-objective. Imagine each piece tied to its neighbours by a strong elastic band. See what happens when you try to advance the technology piece forward more than one place ahead of the others. One of two things will happen. Either the elastic will pull the trailing pieces out of the slots on the pegboard – dislocation and disruption – or the elastic will snap, which means the link between technology and the other two elements is lost.

Dislocation or isolation – they're both bad for business. So we need to re-examine how IT makes new methods of working possible as part of a wider process of business integration.

The core relationship between the four pillars of business integration is: strategy, people, processes and technology, all within a structure which enables, achieves and then sustains improved performance.

In Europe, is the market more sensitised to the need for such a comprehensive process? Do we even see IT being harnessed as a truly integral part of structural change? I don't think so. Why not? Because IT is still viewed too much in isolation. There are several reasons for this.

IT: THE MANAGEMENT GAP

First there is in many European companies a complete divide between chief executives and chief information officers. Indeed, one can detect alarming signs of what is almost a complete abdication of responsibility for IT by general management.

Peter Keen quotes the example of a chief executive at a bank, which spent a great deal of money on computers and was actually a relatively advanced user of IT. And yet this executive confessed: 'To be honest, I'm not familiar with our information-technology strategy'.

Can you imagine *any* CEO saying: 'I'm not familiar with our financial strategy'? 'Our geographic expansion strategy'? 'Our marketing strategy'? Of course not.

And yet that is the situation we have in many of our leading companies: general management see IT as an arcane technical area, akin to the central heating systems of their offices – not as a key part of their business. Plus the IT function in many companies has not been well led. Keen to protect turf and influence, the information system manager has often been the biggest resister of change. Their interests were well served by imposing a management vacuum around their IT empires.

Even where this is not the case, where is the overlap in interests between the information systems (IS) manager and the chief executive? The IS manager is responsible for:

- systems;
- hardware/software;
- operating systems;
- systems architecture;
- IS trends and directions;

- department performance;
- IS budget;
- operations;
- applications; and
- security.

The CEO has a completely different set of responsibilities:

- shareholder value;
- investor/analyst relations;
- vision/mission/strategy;
- image and media relations;
- environment; and
- organisational performance.

We in the IT industry have a role to play in bridging the gap. Many companies, particularly in the United States, have made high profile appointments of chief information officers (CIOs). Perhaps the thought was that they alone could carry IT strategy on their shoulders, thus obviating the need for anyone else to think about it. But many of these high profile appointments are now non-appointments. As *Business Week* stated in 1991, 'CIO might well stand for career is over'.

Something is not working. I suggest it is the process of management, rather than the organisation structure or quality of the CIO management appointments.

IS THE IT INDUSTRY TO BLAME?

We in this industry cannot be entirely proud of our contribution either. Too often we have concentrated on delivering a technology solution which fits a specification, whether it is appropriate or not. Whether it can be used effectively or not. Whether it really serves the business or not.

Too often service vendors have grown their businesses by building a nice cosy relationship with IT directors in their customer companies. Too often senior management did not understand what was going on in their own company. There is a challenge for all of us in this industry which stems from the difficulty of outgrowing our roots.

WE ARE ALL PRODUCTS OF OUR HISTORY

The traditional body-shopper (and many of the largest service providers in Europe grew from this beginning) has tended:

- to look to a rate of return on the individual;
- to maximise profits through very tight financial control over very decentralised operations.

The software vendor thinks in terms of solutions through packaged software. The hardware vendor is dedicated to shifting boxes but, recognising the need for service, is now selling information technology 'solutions'. But there is no such thing as a system solution; only a business solution. The facilities management (FM) supplier is rooted in a history of cost reduction and an unyielding contract. Most of the consulting and accounting firms have challenges too. They are rooted in a history of advising and evaluating rather than doing. These are all far removed from what is necessary to meet today's business problems.

THE NEED FOR NEW PARADIGMS

To break free from the past requires new thinking across a broad front. I suggest that we need five new paradigms in our industry.

New systems paradigms

The typical large company now maintains more than 35 million lines of computer code. Fifty to seventy per cent of a company's programming resources are being spent on maintenance. This unfortunate state of affairs stems from poor design architecture, poor construction and poor maintenance. Companies are wrapped up in many times modified spaghetti code from the distant past.

Looking forward we must re-think totally our system design concepts to accommodate (excuse the lapses into technospeak):

- object orientation;
- re-usability;
- integrated performance support;
- client servers;
- open platforms; and
- business re-engineering methodologies.

Migration and co-existence strategies will be key. The grand design ('scrap everything and start again using a total-information-and-engineering approach to build new data-driven systems which will cope with all future business scenarios') is out. Architectures which are realistic and which will accommodate existing code are in.

That is why our *foundation* case tool is so important to us. It provides a standard yet open architecture for the design of client server processing systems. Increasingly it is at the heart of all software we produce: custom, design-aid components or package.

New time/geography paradigms

The rapid acceleration in the speed with which new technologies are finding their way to the markets, and the reduction in their expected life cycles, has to be reflected in the systems we are building.

The question of geography also has particular relevance to corporations in Europe struggling to keep control over businesses now operating over greater areas and distances. That is why many multinationals want common-core systems which are not geographically constrained but can be rapidly adapted to local requirements. Competitiveness on a world stage now is producing a requirement for world-class solutions, even from institutions that do not compete outside their borders.

New quality paradigm

Traditionally, as in manufacturing, we in the systems business defined quality in terms of conformance. We inspected, through quality assurance, conformance with specification. We have moved on beyond there to the wider aspects of a quality management system as per ISO 9000 guidelines.

Some companies have gone further, as we are doing, by

conducting customer-satisfaction surveys. But this is nothing like enough to ensure real customer satisfaction. In manufacturing, the focus has moved beyond satisfaction to customer delight. And customer delight stems from an improvement to their business – to their ability to serve their customers.

Fundamentally, the quality of a new system has to be measured in terms of its value to the client – and that can only be assessed in terms of the business result it achieves.

Now here's a challenging thought: maybe fees should be related to business results achieved, rather than time spent. This would certainly focus our minds on how to relate IT spending to business results.

A new buying paradigm

The old buying paradigm was to buy input quantities, whether of hardware, software or systems builders. In an attempt to instil some discipline on the explosion of information technology investment, companies imposed traditional purchasing techniques, even traditional purchasing personnel. But to no avail.

If we are to really measure our work by reference to business results achieved, then this fundamentally requires a new joint approach. We need to look at the problem in a re-engineering context. We will only be able to get a proper relationship between us and the clients by a win/win partnership approach, the same as in the best practice in manufacturing.

We need to work in partnership with the client to define and agree how business value is to be achieved and how results should be measured. This has mutual benefit. Massive cost overruns are caused not so much by technological incompetence or poor management (though these have a role) but by fuzzy thinking on the scope and business purpose of the project.

A new supply paradigm

The role of the IT supplier needs re-appraisal as well. The traditional lexicon for our industry has totally collapsed. We are called Andersen Consulting, but our mission is to help our clients change to be more successful.

Our mission is to work in partnership with our client to bring about quantum improvements in performance by harnessing all the elements of strategy, people, processes and technology. The work we are doing with a number of utility companies in Europe, post-privatisation, provides a number of excellent examples of this total change imperative. Also, we are increasingly working in continuous-improvement mode following or alongside major quantum change. Often this involves some type of outsourcing.

In our view, outsourcing has to be much more than cost reduction or financial engineering. In the long term it has to add value through knowledge and experience. For example, in one situation we are managing the configuration management in a very complex co-operative processing environment even though, in this instance, the mainframe computer operations are being handled by a more traditional FM supplier.

An interesting extension of continuous improvement is to outsource business operations – as in the case of BP Exploration – where we have actually acquired 300 accountants from BP Exploration and now run the entire accounting information service for BP Exploration.

In the new supplier paradigm, companies will have to be global in scope and will need a wide scope of functional specialisation. To be a global player you must have significant presence on the ground in every major market. To provide service, as I have defined it, you must have a very wide spread of expertise. This is why we are now seeing a scramble by vendors to extend their scope, both geographically and in terms of service.

Merging people companies is not easy. Moreover, many of these acquisitions will have been expensive. How will the merged companies achieve a sufficient rate of return? I do not know – and am merely thankful that Andersen Consulting has not needed to go down this difficult and dangerous path. Our previous leaders have bequeathed us an inheritance which includes major operations in every European country – as well as deep capabilities in:

- information technology;
- strategic services;
- change management; and
- value-driven process re-engineering.

But whilst the global coverage needs to be wide both to capture world-class solutions and to serve multinationals, the organisational conundrum is to be totally responsive locally, yet at the same time seamlessly integrated where that is required.

Similarly, whilst the technical and functional skills must be very wide, they must also be deep and this means preserving pockets of deep skills. Yet, again, seamlessly integrated where that is needed.

The companies that have had to achieve this global scope by merger will not find it easy to achieve this balance. I know that because even we do not find it easy, despite our common heritage, common methodology, common training and very focused culture.

I was intrigued to read in a *Business Week* article on Tom Peters, the management guru and author, that he is now quoting as examples of successful decentralisation, companies such as Andersen and McKinsey. He says:

> The average decentralised corporation is not decentralised. It is a sham, a sick joke. The best models for the organisation of the future are advertising agencies or consultancies where work is performed by cross-functional project teams that use their collective intellect to satisfy visible customers. Such companies 'trade in pure knowledge'.

Of course, the model of a small single-location consultancy is not easily replicated in a worldwide organisation, in our case, of around 25,000 people. But the fundamentals are the same.

Our key assets are knowledge and people. There is a fundamental difference, in my view, between a company such as our own seeking a financial return on knowledge capital and a hardware or software vendor with a culture oriented to producing a return on financial capital by maximising unit sales.

The knowledge company needs first to recruit the best people. Luckily, in our case, that is not a difficult start. In the UK we had applications from one-third of all people graduating from British universities. But this is only the beginning, we need to invest very heavily in training and experience.

A greater challenge, as the organisation grows, is to maintain the efficiency and effectiveness of our international reach in developing and using key resources.

The challenge is particularly acute in Europe. We are a substantial organisation with fees just over $1 billion and 9,384 people. We must be doing something right – in the year ending 31 August 1992, we grew by a further 17 per cent on top of our growth over the last few years, which has consistently measured over 25 per cent. A remarkable result in the current climate.

But the challenge of adapting ourselves, of making the 'global, yet local' and 'deep, yet integrated' skills work is immense. Like all multinational corporations we are trying to balance every side of the matrix. We are organised simultaneously by industry, by geography and by service line or skill set.

We aim to achieve a certain amount of coherence. Yet at the same time, live with a necessary degree of what author Richard Pascale calls 'contention'.

We have industry leaders, centres of excellence, country missions, functional heads, every type of organisation. Frankly, it looks messy on any organisation chart but then, perhaps, to quote Tom Peters again:

> If the market has gone bonkers, you'd better have a bonkers organisation.

Perhaps it's not such a bonkers organisation. We are, in fact, a truly transnational organisation founded on national partnerships that are bound together into an internationally integrated and interdependent firm. So there is no 'home' country where the majority shareholding resides. We have a single global profit pool so everybody has an interest in the success of the global firm. We all have an interest in re-investing in the business and in fact well over half our profits are re-invested every year.

Our aim is for synergy to occur as naturally as possible so that the organisation works together in all sorts of mysterious ways, but ones which are consistent with delivering what is needed for our clients.

CONCLUSION

I could say that the bloom has indeed faded from the rose of information technology and we have to do something about it. But such a conclusion is not, in itself, adequate.

Information technology is not an end in itself. It has no value in isolation. IT is no more clever than the people, processes and strategies which drive it.

So I should say it's not the rose that's losing its bloom. Maybe it's just that people thought IT was one kind of flower when in fact it is a rather different plant.

We in the service industry have to play the lead in changing this perception. In order to do that we will have to change ourselves.

Vernon Ellis

Vernon Ellis is Managing Partner of Andersen Consulting – Europe. He joined the firm in 1969 after graduating from Oxford University in Philosophy, Politics and Economics. He was one of the first batch of graduates directly recruited into the consulting firm for training in information technology. During most of his career with the firm he has worked with clients in the financial services sector.

His special interest is in the impact of information technology on organisation and strategy development and he has been a speaker at several international conferences. He is on the Board of IMD, Lausanne, Switzerland.

He became a partner in 1979 and from 1986 to 1989 was Managing Partner of Andersen Consulting in the UK. He is currently a member of the Executive Committees of both Andersen Consulting and Arthur Andersen & Co. SC.

Andersen Consulting

Andersen Consulting is a worldwide management and information consulting partnership, with over 25,000 personnel in 151 offices. It is the largest consulting practice of its kind in the world.

Andersen Consulting's presence in Europe dates back to the establishment of practices in Milan, London and Paris in 1957. Today, Andersen Consulting's European practices have revenues of $1,103.4 million. A total of 9,834 professionals operate throughout Europe providing a broad range of management and information technology services; Systems Integration and Systems Management (outsourcing and disaster recovery services); Change Management Services (IT-related management consultancy training) and Strategic Services (general management consulting and IT strategy).

The organisation has expertise and experience across the full spectrum of business needs – strategy, business processes, technology and people. It specialises in the design, construction and installation of large, complex computer-based information systems – and their management and operation when required – for clients in almost every professional, business, industrial and government sector.

Andersen Consulting is the acknowledged leader in the integration of business skills and information technology expertise, providing its clients with effective business solutions to achieve business advantage. The majority of Andersen Consulting's clients are companies in *The Times* Top 200, public utilities or government departments. In 1992, Andersen Consulting's worldwide revenues were $2.72 billion.

9
Payment Systems
Common Knowledge
Charles T Russell
CEO and President,
Visa International

Doing business in Europe is no different than doing business anywhere else in the world. This premise is simple, but not simplistic. From a marketing point of view, Europe is a microcosm of the world. Both are conglomerates of individual, local markets, each market unique in important respects.

The European Community is a common market only in formally defined terms of trade. To the marketing organisation hoping to carve out a pan-European presence, sales in Europe must be generated market by market. For the majority of products and services, markets in Europe are myriad and differ by custom, language, and need. Hence, successful businesses serving Europe have devised means to differentiate their offerings according to the specific, locally determined markets among and within the nations of the European Community.

On the other hand, the need for reduced impediments to cross-border trade is a crying one. And although it will never cause or be confused with cultural homogenisation, the EC's formation is a pragmatic response to economic trends that are bigger than all of Europe.

TRENDS

Trends in telecommunications, travel and investment have combined to render national borders transparent for certain types of commercial transactions and cross-border interchanges. These trends have forged the so-called 'global village,' which recognises the common traits of the diverse markets and cultures that exist simultaneously on this little planet. As such, developments in one market directly or indirectly influence other markets.

However, the fact that we live in a global village does not lessen the challenge. For although our different nations and cultures have been drawn closer together – by telecommunications, by advances in transportation, and by international trade – this new closeness has actually heightened contrasts among locales. These differences are at once the source of conflict and trauma as well as the spice of life.

Nevertheless, as the European Community recognises, in a world knit together by electronics and instantaneous communications, impediments to cross-border trade within a region are uneconomic. Most important, such impediments are uncompetitive in the fast-paced, expanding arena of global trade. The same realisation, of course, has forged other formal and informal regional trading blocs such as the North American Free Trade Agreement, several regional trading groups among the nations of Central and South America, and the informal, high-growth dynamic of intra-regional trade among Asian nations, to cite a few examples.

BUSINESS: LOCAL OR GLOBAL?

Due to the nature of its business, Visa International finds itself on the cusp where the two realities of international business operation intersect:

- market penetration must be achieved at the local level among myriad, diverse cultures; and

- the world is inexorably, albeit slowly and fitfully, evolving toward truly global trade, where individual nations, as they ascend the ladder of economic development, gravitate toward their comparative advantages, *vis à vis* their trading partners.

Visa International has staked its future growth on a pragmatic embrace of these two seemingly contradictory frameworks for international marketing and operation.

WHAT WE DO

Visa International is in the business of consumer payments. Payments represent a unique constellation in the galaxy of consumer-oriented businesses. At the risk of stating the obvious, payment is a fundamental part of every commercial transaction. If commerce is *yin*, payment is *yang*.

The fact that payment is so basic to all forms of commerce, everywhere in the world, has afforded Visa International difficult and extremely valuable lessons in the international marketing of consumer services.

WHAT WE HAVE LEARNED

One of the more difficult lessons we have learned is that the latest issues in financial marketing are among the age-old issues of international marketing. The fundamental puzzle is how to deliver a payment service that functions globally to vastly different cultures through vastly different distribution channels. The seemingly conflicting mandates of local market primacy and global utility are endemic to our every move; they reverberate throughout our organisation.

A look at the Visa organisation's evolution traces our approach to the local/global dichotomy. Our operating structure really manifests our commitment to *both* global *and* local utility.

BACKGROUND

Visa is an unusual organisation, unique in some respects. The membership association that is Visa International did not spring up fully formed, like Athena from the head of Zeus. In 1958, a large regional bank in the United States, Bank of America in California, issued the BankAmericard credit card. This programme was extended internationally through licensing agreements with financial institutions. In 1974, the predecessor of Visa International – IBANCO – was formed. Renamed Visa in 1977, this was a multinational, non-stock membership corporation for administering the Visa programme. Today, Visa is owned by about 18,000 member financial institutions. Our credit and deposit-access (debit) cards are accepted at more than 10 million locations throughout the world. In 1992, our worldwide card transaction volume was more than US$457 billion. We are projecting an increase in that volume to US$1 trillion by the turn of the century. Underscoring the scope of the Visa organisation is the fact that we are the largest purchaser of foreign exchange on a spot basis in the world. So we are big. And our reach is global.

But we are made up of a great many smaller institutions – institutions with strong ties to their local markets. Before the Visa name was adopted, most banks and regions were issuing their own brand of bank cards in their own markets, cards such as the Barclaycard in Britain, Bancomer in Mexico, Carte Bleue in France, and Chargex in Canada. All of these cards had significant local presences in their own markets.

Today, with a stronger global recognition through the Visa mark, these organisations still have significant local presence because they retained flexibility with products appropriate to their local payment cultures. However, the strength of the global Visa brand has vastly increased the utility of their credit and deposit-access card offerings to a global scale.

ORGANISATION

Visa International's membership structure is *multi-domestic*. It is distinct from the typical multinational. The typical multinational exports corporate policies from a single headquarters nation, forcing the same centrally defined product or service on every market, domestic and offshore. Visa, on the other hand, relies on members – local financial institutions who know their local market characteristics first hand – to set their own product, service, and pricing parameters. Thus Visa, down to the very fibre of its organisational structure, gives primacy to local market needs.

Emphasising local market needs over a prefabricated 'global' way of using payment cards, was, in truth, not the result of brilliant marketing theorisation. In fact, it was simply pragmatic.

THE NEED TO RESPECT CULTURAL DIFFERENCES

To pretend that what is good for one payments culture is good for all simply does not work. The payment process is a function embedded too deeply in the cultural consciousness to make any quick sweeping change from one custom, that of pay-as-you-go, say, to that of credit. Or vice versa.

In the world of today, there is no all-encompassing, unified demand for a single payments system. In addition to cultural constraints, payment systems differ from market to market, by economic development levels and, critically, telecommunications and electronic infrastructures. France, for instance, has long nurtured a system of charge and debit with bank cards, but credit card usage in that country is relatively scant. Then, too, France is supporting smart card usage over other payment system configurations that rely on a telecommunications cost structure lower than that available in France. Germany, on the other hand, traditionally has embraced neither credit nor debit, though that mentality is rapidly changing. Other European markets, such as most of those in eastern Europe, have more rudimentary payment systems, low cultural sophistication regarding payments, and telecommunications and electronic infrastructures incapable of supporting all but paper-based card payments. Indeed, throughout Europe generally, telecommunications costs are higher than those in the United States and Canada, by orders of magnitude. And this fundamental environmental difference will result in different evolutionary paths for the payment systems of these regions.

WHERE WE ARE GOING . . . SLOWLY

That is today, not the future. We at Visa have carved out a vision of the future that does indeed rely on a single on-line, real-time, electronic payments system that functions everywhere in the world, replacing cash and cheques everywhere in the world. It is a wonderful vision . . . the more so, because it is achievable. But not tomorrow. Not in the near-term. The truly universal payment system, the cashless society, will be a 21st Century phenomenon.

Because payment is so firmly rooted in the cultural consciousness of a market, it tracks the development of commerce in that market. And this fundamental linkage to commercial trends underlies the genesis of Visa as a global consumer payment system.

VISA VIABILITY

Just as the formation of the European Community has been a pragmatic response to evolving commercial realities, Visa has built its viability as a pragmatic response to the changing commercial habits of consumers. As commerce and travel draw the world more closely together, as international travel becomes increasingly common, it has become imperative to Visa that our card be accepted by merchants anywhere our cardholders travel, that the Visa card be more convenient than cash or cheques.

FOREIGN EXCHANGE

For example, one service for consumers that will become increasingly important as globalisation proceeds is foreign exchange. For travellers to many different countries, the 'haircuts' taken for each currency exchange by a foreign exchange dealer can seriously erode capital. Conversion fees frequently run as high as 7 per cent.

Visa, on the other hand, automatically obtains for the cardholder an interbank exchange rate, far better than what is otherwise available to individuals. And, greatly augmenting the kind of utility consumers are looking for, foreign transactions are all consolidated on the cardholder's one monthly statement, all billed in his or her domestic currency – no matter how many countries were involved.

AUTOMATIC TELLER MACHINES

The most significant thing about our foreign exchange service is the fact that travellers can access their Visa accounts or their personal bank accounts for local currency at more than 150,000 Visa/Plus ATMs in at least 63 countries, 24 hours a day. Visa ATMs are located in more than 90 international airports around the world, including 27 in Europe. In 1992, Visa/Plus ATMs worldwide processed more than 181 million cross-border transactions.

In addition, Visa owns and markets the Plus ATM mark and processes all Plus foreign ATM transactions. Visa/Plus ATMs are located at most US airports and at many major European airports. The combination of Visa and Plus transactions last year exceeded

281 million – the largest for any such network in the world. We recently expanded Visa's ATM utility through an agreement with Eufiserv. Eufiserv ATMs in Germany, Belgium, Spain, and Portugal will soon accept Plus and Visa cards. Eufiserv has almost 22,000 ATMs in Europe, and we expect its members in additional countries to join the Visa/Plus agreement over the next couple of years.

ELECTRONIC FUNDS TRANSFER

We are taking our foreign exchange service a step beyond payments for purchases and electronic funds access. We are developing an electronic service that will allow consumers to transfer funds from their Visa accounts to businesses and individuals in other countries. This cross-border payment service responds to a European Commission report that cited the inefficiencies and inordinate fees for most cross-border consumer payments.

A HUGE POTENTIAL

At Visa, we see travellers and cross-border consumer payments as the wedge market to the new world of payments, where, from the consumer point of view, at least, national borders are transparent. At Visa, we have put a number on the consumer payments market. The 'reasonably available market', to use the trade label, we estimate at about US$8 trillion.

A WAY TO GO YET

However, for the very same reasons that the European common market will not result in cultural homogeneity, the new world of payments – the cashless society – is the end game of an evolutionary process that still has a long way to go. Market expectations that accompany globalisation in the financial markets or the expansion of international trade may push the fast-forward button on technological advancements such as biometrical card-holder identification (retina-scanning and electronic thumbprinting, for example), chip cards, or even home banking. However, nothing other than time will cause the diversity of payments cultures around the world to evolve into one global cashless society.

Since we intend to be a winner in that market of the future, Visa International is currently making major systems investments. We do provide global utility. Our mark is accepted all around the world. We cannot foist technologically advanced infrastructures on all our markets. Rather, our job as a winning business organisation is to find systems solutions that accommodate every infrastructure we encounter everywhere in the world *and* to provide migration paths to more advanced systems that provide greater utility for our merchants, cardholders, and member financial institutions.

While our systems investments allow us to accommodate local payments infrastructures and provide global utility for every Visa card, we have found that establishing a presence in European markets involves more. Building market share in Europe is truly a ground-up endeavour. Our experience has been that brick-and-mortar investments, that is, local offices, are critical to the initial stages of market penetration. And this physical market presence is the basis of our dedication to serving local market needs, to understanding and accommodating the idiosyncrasies of payments specific to individual nations.

CONCLUSION

In summary, woe betide the consumer product organisation that acts as if 'one size fits all' in Europe. Visa International's formula for success in Europe relies on serving local market needs with payments services tailored to meet those needs; *and* on accommodating those locally determined services in the spectrum of our global payment system.

Charles T Russell

Charles T Russell, 62, is chief executive officer and president of Visa International and heads the bankcard association of 18,000 member financial institutions which operate the world's largest consumer card payment system.

Russell was appointed to his current post in May 1984. He joined Visa (then called National BankAmericard, Inc.) in 1971, six months after the company was founded, as vice president for operations. Following that, he served as senior vice president, executive vice president and president and chief operating officer of Visa USA.

Before joining Visa, Russell spent 16 years with Pittsburgh National Bank (PNB). He first served as a management trainee, in 1953, after his discharge from the US Army. He then held a series of management positions until he was appointed to start up PNB's bank card operation, one of the earliest in the USA, in 1965. PNB later became one of the founding members of Interbank, the predecessor of MasterCard International. In 1969, Russell left PNB to operate and manage the Master Charge programme for Wachovia National Bank and Trust Company in Winston-Salem, NC.

Currently he serves on the board of directors for Interlink, Plus System, Inc., and the University of Pittsburgh's Joseph M Katz School of Business.

Russell, a native of Pittsburgh, PA, earned Bachelor's degrees in business administration from the University of Pittsburgh and the Stonier Graduate School of Banking.

Visa International

Visa International is a multi-domestic financial industry organisation. Best known for its credit and debit cards, Visa is owned not by stockholders in a conventional sense, but by its members – more than 18,000 banks and financial institutions around the world. This is why Visa calls itself multi-domestic and not multinational. Wherever Visa cards are issued, it is done by a domestic organisation.

As the most widely recognised consumer payment system in the world, Visa provides over 10 million merchant locations and more than 300 million cardholders with superior payment products, services and delivery-systems performance.

To give an idea of the magnitude of the Visa payment system, in 1991, the global collective sales volumes of the top ten worldwide car makers were less than Visa International. The same is true of the top ten oil companies. If Visa International had been a country in 1991, and its payment service volume was measured as gross domestic product, it would have ranked as the 10th largest country in the world.

By the year 2000, the Visa payment system will accommodate more than US$1 trillion in transactions annually, nearly twice as much as the 1992 volume.

Visa's vision is to become the first truly accepted global payment system.

10

Pharmaceuticals

'Mirror, Mirror, on the Wall' ... Shaping the Image of the Pharmaceutical Industry

Henry Wendt
Chairman,
SmithKline Beecham PLC

IMAGE PROBLEMS

The current image of the prescription pharmaceutical industry is poor. The public's understanding and evaluation of this business now ranks it close to the bottom in most opinion surveys, in terms of perceived social responsibility and contribution to the common good. We seem to have displaced the oil and chemical industries as the industrial sector held in the least esteem.

Worse, our products, many of which are truly miraculous in their efficacy, are now thought to be overpriced, or to put it another way, to represent less value than our customers pay for. In a recent survey in the United States, only one out of five respondents thought prescription pharmaceutical products represented value for money. This really hurts since we have always believed that our products were our best salesmen.

And finally, as we all know, the public perception of our industry is continuing to deteriorate. The trend is down. Public confidence is dropping and political leaders grasping for solutions to extremely difficult and complex problems are quick to identify and excoriate demons believed to be vulnerable by lack of public or political support.

WIDESPREAD INDUSTRY CRITICISM

In the United States the newly elected president, practising a late 20th-century version of populist politics, has singled out the pharmaceutical industry for vitriolic criticism. Not at all coincidentally, this criticism has been accompanied by media exposés in a number of city newspapers – Boston, New York and Philadelphia – and Congressional hearings are being conducted in the manner of a kangaroo court. In the fine tradition of American politics, these are usually the precursor to the introduction of punitive legislation.

GOVERNMENT REACTIONS

The voices are certainly more strident in the USA. There is nothing new about that! But the themes – the opinion polls, the politics and the image of the industry – are remarkably common throughout the developed world. In fact, the political expression of the deteriorating image of the pharmaceutical industry first became apparent in Germany, where a Christian Democratic government forced reference pricing into an ailing health-care system. This in a country with a tradition of free-market economics and a strong, internationally competitive pharmaceutical industry.

They were widely applauded for doing so. The political vulnerability of the industry in Germany did not go unnoticed elsewhere. The Netherlands followed and now the Nordic countries have announced similar measures.

Even in Great Britain, where the industry is generally held in somewhat higher repute, the Government, groping for budgetary Band Aids, announced an arbitrary 'limited list' in the midst of renegotiation of the entire pharmaceutical price regulation scheme. The pharmaceutical industry in Canada and Australia has been virtually disenfranchised and Italy has taken draconian measures to reduce the pharmaceutical portion of the health-care budget.

A GLOBAL/LOCAL PROBLEM

In short, the themes of disenchantment and discontent with the pharmaceutical industry are global and are remarkably consistent around the world. They revolve primarily around issues of value for money and the socially responsible nature of industry practices. The expression of the themes, of course, is local; sometimes intensely local at the physician, hospital and patient level, but it is also national and essentially political.

A NEW SOCIAL CONTRACT

We seem to be witnessing a situation in which society is bent on renegotiating the terms of its social contract with the pharmaceutical industry. Paradoxically, the demand for a new social contract is occurring at a time when the industry has never been more successful, as measured by several factors:

- the safety and efficacy of products recently brought to market;
- the promise of products in the development pipelines;
- the quality of its science;
- the capacity to innovate truly advanced therapy for diseases or conditions as yet impossible to treat;
- the patent protection accorded to its intellectual property;
- the financial results delivered to its investors; and
- at least until recently, its market capitalisation on the major stock exchanges of the world.

What has gone wrong? How could one of the great industrial engines of innovation and contributors to the quality of life suffer so badly in the eyes of those who benefit so much from its effort? And what can be done about it?

WHAT WENT WRONG

The prescription pharmaceutical industry has always been intensely introverted. Proud and even self-admiring but always introverted.

When I joined SmithKline & French Laboratories nearly 40 years ago, our corporate credo read 'in the service of medicine'. By medicine, we meant the medical profession. We communicated with physicians and no one else. In fact, we literally tried to hide from the public at large behind the white gowns of practising physicians. The logic was that the physician made the decision of which product to use and therefore the physician was the customer. The patients received our products repackaged by pharmacists and knew absolutely nothing about the contents other than minimal instructions for their use. We had no public relations whatsoever – only professional relations – and we fervently hoped that we didn't have a public image of any kind. Indeed, as events proved we were successful. We had no real image in the public eye whatsoever!

That 'professional phase' of our public image – and our social contract – ended 30 years ago with the passage of the 1962 Food & Drug amendments in the United States, establishing a new benchmark of regulation to rigorous standards of safety and efficacy. The FDA standards for evidence of safety and efficacy spread around the world. They were sometimes adapted with a pragmatic philosophy, as in Great Britain, but usually were applied with bureaucratic zeal under the rubric that regulation is good and more must be better.

Its worth recalling that the 1962 Food & Drug Amendments were proposed as legislation by the Tennessee senator Estes Kefauver, on the back of the thalidomide tragedy. In the process, Senator Kefauver attacked the pharmaceutical industry with religious zeal. He found an easy victim as his target. It was an industry totally unprepared to defend itself and one without friends or allies.

Senator Kefauver rewrote the social contract replacing trust in the pharmaceutical companies and indirectly trust in the medical profession, with trust in regulation. Although thalidomide was a safety issue, he used the occasion to demand scientific verification of efficacy as well as safety by a strong regulatory agency. The public transferred its trust from physicians and the pharmaceutical companies to the national regulatory agency. Costs went up, the time to bring a product to market lengthened, and products which could not satisfy the new rigorous standards came off the market. During this stage of history which we might label as the 'regulatory phase', the pharmaceutical industry adapted and went on to prosper mightily as companies expanded around the world and exploding knowledge in the biological sciences brought forth wonderful new products.

Throughout this phase the same introverted tendencies continued. For the most part, we have chosen to let our products speak for us to the public. Even the occasional institutional advertisements run by individual companies or trade associations feature our products as spokespersons.

FINANCIAL CLOUT

The one major exception was that with growth and financial success, we shed our introverted tendencies with respect to the financial markets. We became eloquent spokesmen in describing, especially in financial terms, our scientific and commercial triumphs. And we were rewarded. Our companies were accorded huge price/earnings premiums and gigantic market capitalisations. We became the darlings of Wall Street and the City. Investor relations became much more important than public relations. The primacy of the shareholder in the hierarchy of executive priorities was clear. And for the leading companies, the shareholder was often adoring. Introversion was transformed to narcissism. We came to believe we really were beautiful and were certain that everyone would think so too.

WHERE WE ARE NOW

During the 'regulatory phase', which takes us to the present, the destiny of our industry seemed to be in the hands of both the regulatory agencies who made the 'life and death' decisions regarding our products and the financial markets who scored our managerial performance. In many respects, these two quite different arbiters made, or at least guided, the decisions and the conduct of the industry. If the agencies and the markets were happy, we were happy and, incidentally, quite well rewarded.

What went wrong? We forgot about our customer. In fact, we were less than clear about who our customer was.

It's interesting that even now the mission statements of most of our companies express dedication to the patient, a customer who takes the medicine but who rarely pays the bill. The logic is that although he or she does not make the purchase decision, it is the patient who benefits from the attributes of the product. The physician is now seen as one of several intermediaries.

I have yet to see a corporate mission statement in which the customer is defined as the insurer, the government or the taxpayer. Yet it is obvious that the usual definition of customer is the one who pays. The one who pays generally insists on making the purchase decision.

TRADE ASSOCIATIONS AS VOICE

To the extent that we conversed with the one paying the bills at all, we did so through our national trade associations. They walked the corridors of government, fending off harmful actions and advocating informed and positive treatment. Our national trade associations to a very significant degree were the voice of the industry to our real customer – the one who pays. More than anything else we are now witnessing the ascendancy of the ultimate customer.

THE PACE OF CHANGE QUICKENS

How could this happen to such a great and wonderful industry? We live in a world of change. There is nothing new about change, but what is new is the pace of change. Signs of rapid change abound but perhaps nowhere as much as in the life sciences, the very root of our industry. Technological change and its instant communication is one of the major drivers for change in our global society. Knowledge is exploding at an exponential rate – it is thought to be doubling every 18 months – and it is pushing change everywhere. The ability to provide health care and the demand for health care is exploding at a similar rate. The appetite for health care and for our products is outstripping the ability to finance it and is placing great strain on health-care systems in all societies.

Governments respond in curious ways: closing big city hospitals in the face of rising demand, for example; slashing medical research budgets in an era of unprecedented discovery as another example; and lashing out at the most productive and cost effective component of the health-care system, the pharmaceutical industry, as yet another example.

As you would expect in this environment characterised by rapid change, society's agenda as regards the pharmaceutical industry has also changed. It has changed rapidly and with decisiveness. Safety and efficacy – the dominant theme of the regulatory phase –

are now mostly taken for granted. The public today wants access, knowledge and most of all, assurance of economic value. And they want these attributes from an industry that displays a sound sense of social responsibility.

Some of us may have sensed change in society's agenda but all of us failed to reorder our priorities. We continued to worship the gods of the regulatory agencies and the financial markets. Of course, they continue to be important but we now must find a central place on the altar for the customer who pays the bills.

As society changed its agenda, the representatives of the industry – the national trade associations – were in constant contact with the customer who pays the bills: the national governments. Ironically, trade associations are least sensitive to change. Their mission is usually to defend the *status quo*. In fact, the one thing they can always get all their members to agree on is the positive attributes of the *status quo*. And there is great virtue in that. It is correct and probably desirable that the associations defend and act for the *status quo*. But that does not excuse leaders of the major companies from sensing change and reordering their priorities. Their priorities will then be understood and find expression by the trade associations.

WHAT CAN WE DO TO IMPROVE THINGS?

Let me set forth an agenda for the leaders of the industry, the executives of the large, globe-spanning, research-based companies. As industry leaders they can make their weight felt. Eventually their views and activities will alter the terrain of discussion.

In the first instance, we must demonstrate a willingness to embrace change externally just as we manage change internally. We must redefine our customers to include those that pay the bills. As with any customer, we must understand their needs and match our products and services accordingly. First and foremost, we must be sure our organisations fully understand and accept and act on this redefinition of the customer.

In designing the match to the customer's needs we must help solve their problems. We must go beyond our products to find ways to constructively help resolve the tremendous stress caused by the enormous demands for health care and the finite resources to provide it. In other words, we must address the current stresses and strains in the health-care systems on our customer's terms, not merely with our narrow industry concerns.

We must manage our public affairs the way we manage our businesses. As global companies, we must recognise the global themes that are defining the new social contract and respond to them on a global basis. We must develop information and programmes that constructively address the global themes. Equally important, we must communicate and implement the global themes on a local basis with exquisite sensitivity and care for each nation's particular circumstance. And we must dedicate the same quality and quantity of management attention and resources to the customer who pays that we do to shareholders and regulatory agencies.

THE RESULTS

The general principles I have outlined will help reorient our industry leadership toward a new social contract. With the power of their organisations lined up behind them and a long-range plan for global strategy and local implementation, society will recognise the industry welcomes change and is ready to participate as a partner in health-care not merely as a distant and aloof supplier.

A CHANGE IN VALUES

But there is also a more specific agenda. We must recognise that safety and efficacy are now commonly taken for granted. This is a mixed blessing in that society has lost sight of the risk/reward ratio so that when unexpected adverse reactions do occur they are thought to be the consequence of some form of malevolent subterfuge or at best incompetence. Nevertheless, the new dimension is that of demand for proof of economic value in addition to therapeutic value. Accordingly, it is incumbent upon our industry to marshal our resources to provide the technology and independent certifiable proof of economic value. Just as our shareholders want proof that our accounting is correct and valid, our customers want proof of value. We should be happy – truly enthusiastic – to provide it.

A CHANGE IN STANDARDS

Our challenge in doing so is to help people understand that it is virtually impossible to design valid cost-effectiveness studies until a product is approved for safety and efficacy and placed on the market. It must not become a requirement for registration. But it is crucial to our future that we respond to the added dimension of proof of value and that we present sound ways of satisfying it.

We must quickly raise the standards of industry conduct – commercial and scientific behaviour – to the highest possible level. The truth is that despite good intentions and high motives, our behaviour doesn't measure up to the requirements of an informed and sceptical society. Every time the FDA requires a 'Dear Doctor' letter redressing wrong promotional behaviour, the entire industry loses a measure of credibility. Every time the press reports a medical symposium conducted in one of the world's great watering spots with expenses paid by a major drug company, the entire industry loses a measure of credibility. We can no longer afford these losses in public esteem. In terms of public trust, we are running out of credit.

PARTNERING

We must meet with our partners in health care – the professions, the policy makers, the insurers and the patients – to fuse our expertise with theirs to design more efficient and responsive systems. This process is no different than meeting with our suppliers and employees to improve the efficiency and productivity of our manufacturing plants and logistical systems. We do it every day and we do it well. If we can't work together with our health-care partners to improve the efficiency and productivity of our health-care systems, we will be relegated to the role of just another cost factor.

COMMUNICATION AND KNOWLEDGE

We live in an age of information. The public wants to know, and has the right to know, essential information about our products. Indeed until they do know, they cannot be expected to be understanding or sympathetic.

Even more fundamentally, it is important that the public understand that much of what we make and sell as products is really information. Information about the active ingredients, what they do and don't do, what risks are associated, what instructions must be followed, what results can be expected, what adverse reactions might occur – in short everything that can be known, must be known. That is why drug development costs about three times more than drug discovery. And it is why pharmaceutical marketing is so expensive and so important. Much, perhaps most, of what is labelled – in mistaken application of business school terminology – as marketing, is dissemination of essential information about the active ingredient. In effect, each tablet and capsule contains both the hardware and software to achieve a therapeutic result.

All our customers – including those who take our products and those who pay for them – should have access to the software element of our products as much as the hardware. It is time to shed the antiquated notion that only health-care professionals have the competency to understand pharmaceutical products.

We can learn much from the terrible tragedy of AIDS. Many AIDS patients know as much or more about the disease and possible therapy as their physicians. As they learn more, they take better care of themselves, adapting their life styles and habits to their condition. Knowledge enables them to take responsibility for their care. They become less of a burden on the health-care system. Their use of pharmaceutical products is informed and rational. They demand information and they use it intelligently and usually in a cost-effective manner. And in doing so, they become strong allies in the relentless search for innovation.

There is, of course, the need for improved communications from our industry, but we know that a good image cannot be purchased from an advertising or public relations agency. We are dealing fundamentally with a matter of public trust. Trust must be earned by performance.

CONCLUSION

I have suggested that we are entering a new phase in our relationship with society. As we approach the challenge of meeting society's agenda in a way which regains public trust, we would do well to relinquish our old habit of introversion replacing it with a genuine desire to reach out to embrace other points of view and others' needs. We must turn away from the mirror and look through the window to the people we serve and who define our continuing contract with the societies we serve. Perhaps the next phase will be labelled by future historians as the 'value' phase. If so, we should seize the chance. There is no doubt about the ability of the pharmaceutical industry to deliver real value in economic as well as therapeutic terms.

Much more than in previous periods of scrutiny, change and transition, we are well positioned to meet the changing needs to our customers and society at large. I am quite confident about the ability – especially the ability of the next generation – of executives and leaders to reorder their priorities and lead the industry to new heights of social and financial performance.

Henry Wendt

Henry Wendt is Chairman of the Board of SmithKline Beecham, a company formed by the 1989 merger of SmithKline Beckman and the Beecham Group. He plans to retire in April 1994, concluding a career which spans more than 35 years with SmithKline Beckman and its predecessor companies. He was named CEO of SmithKline Beckman in 1982 and Chairman in 1987.

A graduate of Princeton University, he has lived and worked in Japan, Britain, Canada and the United States.

Henry Wendt is a member and former Chairman (1988–90) of the US-Japan Business Council and a member of the Trilateral Commission. He is Board Director of Atlantic Richfield Company, Allergan, Inc. and Beckman Instruments, Inc. He is on the Boards of Trustees of the Home Farm Development Trust, a British charitable trust that provides homes and work for the mentally disabled; the Philadelphia Museum of Art and the American Enterprise Institute, a Washington, DC, 'think tank'.

He is the author of *Global Embrace*, a book on the role of transnational corporations in the global economy, published by Harper Business in 1993. He divides his time between Philadelphia, London and his winery, Quivira Vineyards, in Northern California, although he did sail his 43-foot cutter across the Atlantic in 1992.

SmithKline Beecham

SmithKline Beecham was formed in July 1989 through the merger of SmithKline Beckman and the Beecham Group.

Over the years, scientists from both companies have been responsible for a number of notable discoveries. For example, the Beecham research laboratories at Brockham Park became world famous when, in 1957, the penicillin nucleus 6-APA was isolated, enabling the creation of an infinite number of penicillins that could be targeted at a predetermined range of bacteria.

In 1989, a former SmithKline scientist, Sir James Black, was awarded the Nobel Prize for his research that included 'Tagamet', the first effective peptic ulcer treatment, which became available in the UK in 1976. SmithKline was also the first company to market a genetically engineered human vaccine for protection against hepatitis-B.

In 1992, the company had sales of over £5.2 billion, making it one of the world's leading health-care companies. It invested £478 million in research and development (R&D) in that year. It sells over 300 branded products in 130 countries. It has approximately 54,000 employees worldwide (5,000 in R&D alone), and is headquartered in Brentford, just outside London.

11
Property

The Future of the Real Estate Market

Stuart Lipton
Chief Executive,
Stanhope Properties PLC

Business, by its very nature, is in a constant state of evolution. In recent years, for example, financial services and motor manufacturing have been forced to adapt to changing markets. They have become leaner, more efficient and more customer-responsive. Likewise, the computer industry is now going through great change as some of the lumbering hardware giants recognise the success of the smaller, more flexible software houses, and the needs of their customers. Whether the impetus comes from government policy, foreign competition or simply the recognition of out-of-date practices, the result is the same – restructured business with new supplier-buyer relationships.

THE BUSINESS SERVICE INDUSTRY

As we survey the trends and prospects across Europe for the 1990s, it is clear which industries have shaped up for the emerging markets, and which have yet to do so. A key area for change will be the 'business service' industry. Law and accountancy are two potential areas. The real estate business will also undergo a fundamental shift, and I believe it is no exaggeration to say that a new industry will emerge. The new industry will offer a better product to its customers that contributes to productivity and worker welfare. It will offer greater comparability across national boundaries to match global businesses. And it will provide a service which satisfies the various aspirations of its customers.

Property is often regarded simply as a cost of doing business. I believe that property has a more fundamental role in business by providing the right working environment for a company, reflecting its corporate culture and making a positive contribution to its success.

At Stanhope, we have devised a product that is fit for the new market. In the same way that companies such as BMW package and provide warranties for their products in a range of easily-recognised and tailored specifications, we have defined a product that offers certainty, quality and value – all wrapped in a professional development service. Our experience in achieving this, I believe, points to broader lessons for the development, and indicates what type of industry is emerging from the current malaise.

A TIME FOR CHANGE

In many ways, the real estate market has changed in the post-war period. Building technology has changed; planning policies have changed and the uses to which buildings are put have changed. But the basic transaction-based triumvirate of investor, developer and intermediary (broker) has persisted. This culture has dictated a supply-led market which has rarely obliged developers to understand the needs of their customers.

This arrangement worked to a logic that demanded buildings take on a particular form, what we in London call 'vanilla space'. In the 1970s, vanilla meant the dull buildings whose purpose was to secure an income stream for the landlord rather than meet the demands of the occupier. In the 1980s, the criteria were the same, only the marble finish was different.

Investors have dictated building specifications which have protected investment value rather than use value. Since little research was undertaken on the needs of occupiers, the usual result was unfriendly and inefficient buildings, often in the wrong location. Without proper research, the industry failed to keep abreast of trends in the use of office space.

At Stanhope, we have shown the way. Continental developers looked on as we began to place great emphasis on research, to provide occupiers with buildings that match their organisational needs. For example, at Broadgate in the City of London, we researched nearly 100 financial services companies in 1984–85 to understand how their businesses were changing and how this would affect their needs for accommodation. This was the first research of its kind, and it allowed us to provide buildings that precisely matched the needs of post-Big Bang securities houses. Six of the companies we interviewed also became occupiers of our buildings – demonstrating the commercial value of research.

CYCLICAL MARKETS

Partly because investment patterns ignored the needs of users, the market also became highly cyclical. Periods of relative undersupply pushed rents and costs upwards and were routinely followed by oversupply as developers responded to the opportunity to meet unsatisfied demand and capitalise on rising values. This destructive cycle has come to be widely accepted as 'normal'. Until now.

The pattern of speculative development in which the 'let 'em and forget 'em' approach was prevalent is being seriously challenged. Significantly, the challenge is coming from the occupier. Consequently, the UK slump of the early 1990s has set the scene for a major reappraisal of the way real estate is supplied. And this reappraisal is not unique to the UK.

The inefficiencies that have afflicted the property industry (which contributes 12 per cent to national GDP in the UK) will be untenable in the emerging economy of the mid-1990s and beyond in many parts of Europe. Low or reduced inflation, restricted money supply and a growing sense of social responsibility will all encourage expertise and professionalism.

The inefficiency results partly from the fact that the many professions and skills involved in the supply of real estate have become confused about the roles that each serves. And because the suppliers themselves are confused, the customer has grown sceptical and wary. It is my belief that the supply industry must make itself more efficient, more easily understandable and more useful.

LEARNING FROM ELSEWHERE

To understand how the property industry might respond, it is useful to look at other industries tackling similar issues. Three examples best mirror our attempts at Stanhope to approach property development more effectively.

The first is British Petroleum, which is pioneering a new procurement route that is designed to cut the cost of construction work in the North Sea. Based on the partnering principle, BP has created an alliance with its professional service providers and contractors to get away from the traditional adversarial roles so common in our industry today. BP will build closer, longer-term relationships with the client, which will lead to cost benefits and better solutions through co-operation.

The second example is that of Mercedes-Benz in Stuttgart. Its new CEO, Helmut Werner, was recently quoted as saying that the company has accepted that 'radical changes in the world car market mean that Mercedes-Benz will no longer be able to demand premium prices for its products based on an image of effortless superiority'.

If the company were to continue to over-engineer its products, he said, it would be priced out of its markets. Instead of developing the ultimate car and then charging a correspondingly sky-high price as in the past, Werner is moving to a policy of 'target pricing'. Mercedes will decide what the customer is willing to pay in a particular product category – priced against its competitors – and then will cost every part and component to bring in the vehicle at the target price.

The third example is IBM, where a changing market has forced fundamental restructuring. What has been referred to as the world's most successful marketing organisation based its business strategy on the mainframe – the market share for which fell 80 per cent between 1974 and 1984. As one commentator observed: 'The leviathan did not keep up. IBM forgot what made it successful – listening to customers and looking after them.'

What are the lessons for the way we think about property? BP demonstrates that traditional adversarial relationships can be overcome to gain significant benefits. At Stanhope, we use a similar approach in our management of professional teams. In so doing we have achieved cost savings against 'the going rate' of up to 30 per cent, significantly faster delivery times and excellent labour relations.

In the Mercedes-Benz example, replace 'car' with 'building' and you have a ready-made strategy for the property industry. For too long, the property industry at large has provided buildings without regard for the needs of targeted users and which have recently tended to be over-specified. At Stanhope we use value engineering at the design stage to provide high quality buildings that can be shown to provide value for money to occupiers. Furthermore, we have learned the value of targeting with appropriate product.

The IBM lesson must be: do not lose touch with your markets or blindly believe that today's assumptions will serve tomorrow's markets. Stanhope is continuously researching its existing and potential markets to develop a product that matches the changing needs of business. The crucial aspect of forming longer-term relationships with occupiers, of course, is that we stay in touch with changing requirements, and be more able to satisfy needs as they arise.

OCCUPIERS AND PROPERTY

Property, like any other market, works through a balance of supply and demand. As the traditionally supply-led industry yields to one more fairly balanced towards the occupier, such relationships will see the two sides come closer together. The key area where this applies is in the mutual understanding of how business strategy meets property strategy.

The 1980s was a period of rapid growth and change for business generally in most parts of Europe. Expansion and diversification spread as the 'bigger is better' philosophy grew. Planning and decision-making were short term, over-capacity grew and corporate emphasis was on short-term growth rather than on long-term strategy. Property was rarely considered of strategic corporate importance.

Rapid growth meant that businesses actually had the means to subsidise the property industry. Big companies could afford the escalation in rents demanded by landlords. Few questions were asked about the cost or the long-term utility of buildings, either by the providers or the occupiers. The role of property in corporate planning was poorly understood, and its management was a highly reactive process.

Corporate management objectives throughout Europe are very different from those of the 1980s. Economic pressures have forced many companies to examine their cost bases, reduce overheads and improve productivity. Companies in the UK as well as on the Continent have been forced to restructure and adopt new technology. Decision-making and planning are thus focusing on ways to help companies adapt and succeed in increasingly competitive markets.

The implications for property are clear. Occupiers now require buildings that offer value for money and contribute to corporate goals by providing efficient and cost-effective space. More effective use of space will be demanded, and this is likely to lead to a broader adoption of 'cost per employee' as a yardstick of efficiency rather than 'cost per square foot'. Office space will increasingly be regarded as one element in the production process, along with capital goods and labour, for which sophisticated measures of performance will be devised.

One area of new performance measures will be productivity. Worldwide, productivity in the service sector has lagged behind that in manufacturing. Premises have largely been perceived as a cost of doing business. Increasingly, corporate management philosophy is regarding premises as a resource to be managed and utilised with the effectiveness of personnel and capital. This change in mood will mean greater demands on the suppliers of buildings to provide product that reflects increasingly important objectives in terms of, for example, cost, efficiency and value for money.

THE FUTURE OF PROPERTY DEVELOPMENT

Property development, certainly in the post-war period, has been tarnished in most European countries with the image of casino speculation. In part this is caused by a stock of town centres and office blocks, much of which is widely despised. The popular perception is one in which the developers have taken every short cut in order to maximise profit at the expense of quality for the user. There is little defence to be offered.

I have learned, however, that it is possible to provide high quality real estate while at the same time maximising commercial success. I characterised this some years ago with the comment that 'good architecture is good business'. This belief has underpinned our development activity at Stanhope. Quality is a state of mind: it cannot be bolted on like an optional extra. The pursuit of quality must be integral to every part of the development process.

From our first projects at Broadgate in the City of London and at Stockley Park, Europe's leading business park, we have sought to define a new approach to development. This approach, I believe, points the way to the future. It is about defining the needs of occupiers and providing for their needs with buildings which offer clean, efficient space that is cost effective while also being built to a very high quality standard.

The indulgent and over-specified buildings of the 1980s are being replaced with lean buildings. The new occupier is beginning to realise that high quality does not have to mean high cost and that cost does not equal value. Creating world-class buildings means understanding how value relates to the user. At the same time, the buildings are being designed to maximise their value as tradeable assets. This is central to the creation of real estate which does not constrain organisational flexibility in changing markets.

Buildings can contribute to productivity, efficiency, staff morale and corporate culture. Research that we have undertaken on law firms, for example, demonstrates the high value that new entrants to the profession place on the quality of their work environment.

Buildings can also be inexpensive to run, adaptable and flexible to changing needs. If a building is expensive to design and build, the chances are that it will be expensive and difficult to manage.

I believe that offices will come to mirror hotels, by providing user-friendly meeting places, where service is central and there are facilities to support business activity. It is not just about the building: a sense of place is important, together with a mix of work and amenity. Buildings must be part of a safe and secure environment – part of their local community – with provision for leisure facilities.

Development must also respond to the need for more judicious use of resources. For example, much greater emphasis must be placed on taking development to transport rather than transport to development. Why allow inaccessible areas to expand when major opportunities already exist near public transport?

Development in the future will involve much closer relationships between suppliers and users of buildings. While speculative development will undoubtedly return in some form, the new market will offer much greater opportunities for occupiers to procure their space on a more bespoke basis. This will be achieved by working in partnership with chosen suppliers. The United States is already accustomed to this approach. There it is called the build-to-suit market, and the process is more akin to just-in-time delivery than our own laborious and adversarial process. We in Europe must do likewise.

In the 1980s we introduced 'shell and core' development to the UK, whereby occupiers took buildings in their 'shell' state rather than fitted out. This saved time and money for both developer and occupier. However, given closer relationships between suppliers and occupiers, the 1990s is likely to see this replaced by full-service development. Buildings will be fully specified by the occupier from the outset, so that the building can be delivered in an integrated process – packaged and warranteed. The result is excellence in the end product because it has resulted from the input of the end user, as well as the experience of the professional supplier. Stanhope has completed a number of such projects for occupiers such as the UK's Independent Television News; Reuters; BAT, Glaxo and Tetra-Laval.

Better performance measures will become more important. Expertise is back in business and occupiers will become more demanding of the development industry.

Development requires a fully integrated approach, led by a professional developer who is able to add value in the procurement process, and manage development to achieve quality in design and construction and manage risk and complexity in the delivery process.

In Britain, we have been in recession for three years, and project financing has dried up. Occupiers are in a stronger position to determine their own needs and consequent building solutions. The challenge is to provide buildings which have both a long-term commercial value and a long-term use value. This will apply in other European markets as they follow their own recovery cycles.

The 'let 'em and forget 'em' era has passed. Likewise do-it-yourself solutions are a feature of the past. Expertise is once again fashionable and the role of the professional developer is becoming clear. Rather than erecting buildings on speculation, then finding occupiers to pay rent, the developer of tomorrow, including

Stanhope, is more likely to stay away from equity ownership. Borrowing rates are more attractive for most occupiers than for most developers. The development manager of the 1990s will mediate between the investment side and the user side. Working with corporate occupiers, developers can use their expertise to add value, improve efficiency and reduce costs. This represents the full service developer.

Stuart Lipton

Stuart Lipton served as joint chief executive of London's Greycoat Group from 1978 to 1983, during which he oversaw several major developments. In 1983 he was appointed chief executive of Stanhope Properties PLC. Under his direction, Stanhope has built Stockley Park, Broadgate, Ludgate and Chiswick Park, all in the UK.

Mr Lipton also serves as a trustee of the Whitechapel Art Gallery and of the Architecture Foundation. He is a Commissioner of the Royal Fine Art Commission and an adviser to Glyndebourne Productions Ltd. for the development of a new opera house.

Stanhope Properties PLC

In the ten years of its existence, Stanhope Properties has been a driving force within the British property industry. The company has concentrated on a small number of high profile development projects, primarily in the London area. All combine the highest standards of design with the most advanced construction techniques and extensive research.

In 1991, Stanhope and its partners let more space in the City of London than any other developer. The company has begun to expand its interests beyond the UK, starting with the opening of an office in Berlin. Stanhope is actively looking at opportunities to export its development expertise to mainland Europe.

Stanhope had been widely credited with pioneering North American construction and construction management techniques in the UK and setting new standards for building design. The company has commissioned work from some of the world's leading architects and designers, including Norman Foster, Terry Farrell, Richard Rogers and Eric Parry. Stanhope has also led the way in commissioning research into the needs of potential occupiers and in working closely with communities in which its developments are located. It has also been instrumental in establishing environmental guidelines and safety and training standards for the building industry in the UK.

Stanhope's developments are notable for including public art and public spaces as integral parts of the overall scheme. The value of the public art collection at Broadgate has been put at over £3.5 million. Broadgate also features the UK's only outdoor ice rink and an extensive programme of free entertainment.

12
Sporting Apparel
It's Not Just Shoes!

John Duerden
President,
Reebok International Division

For many decades the market in sports footwear was dominated by that most unglamourous of items, the lowly plimsoll, with its vulcanised sole and canvas upper, which came to symbolise physical education for generations of reluctant school children.

It was not until the 1960s that the German Adi Dasler created his revolutionary fusion of branding and sports promotion, signing up leading athletes and sponsoring teams to provide the ultimate endorsement of Adidas shoes, and, naturally, shirts.

Today's athletic footwear market, and indeed the whole vast sportswear industry, are in many ways the result of that pioneering approach, which turned the Adidas trefoil trademark into a badge of success on the shoes and shirts of top sportsmen and women.

There are now three key players in the global sportswear market, Adidas, Nike and Reebok. Currently Nike controls around 30 per cent of athletic footwear sales in the USA, as against 26 per cent for Reebok. In terms of total global sales, the figures are even closer, with Nike at 18 per cent and Reebok just one per cent behind – having displaced Adidas last year to gain the position of number two in the world.

Adidas, at one time the international leader, still outsells both of its main competitors in Europe, but has never made serious inroads into the giant North American market.

Apart from the three big players, a host of lesser brands compete for market share – some long-established names drifting into decline, other newer enterprises establishing small but lucrative niches in a burgeoning marketplace.

The scale of the competition is set into context by considering some more vital statistics. The market for branded athletic footwear is currently worth around $6 billion in the USA, plus another $7 billion in the rest of the world. These figures are based on wholesale prices, and the totals can be roughly doubled to arrive at the retail value.

In fact, athletic footwear now makes up 40 per cent of all shoes sold in the USA, and generations of people have never worn anything else throughout school, college and adulthood.

SHOES AND BEYOND

The potential rewards are even richer for a company such as Reebok which is also heavily involved in producing branded sports clothing – the market for which is probably twice as large again as that for footwear.

With such enormous gains at stake, Reebok has set out to capitalise on its strengths in the USA, in Europe and throughout the world. In order to understand these strengths let us look at the way the company has developed to its present size and status.

HUMBLE BEGINNINGS

Reebok's record of international success would have astonished J W Foster, the Lancashire cobbler who became a celebrated maker of running shoes in the industrial town of Bolton during the last years of Queen Victoria's reign.

Despite its lowly beginnings, the firm established an early reputation for technological innovation. Edwardian athletes soon found that donning Foster's newly-invented running spikes gave them a valuable edge over their rivals, and helped them to exploit their speed and ability to the full.

The message sent loud and clear by Adidas in the 1960s, and later by Nike, was not lost on Joe Foster, a descendant of the Bolton boot-maker, who was keen to exploit the potential of the market with a more exciting range of products and a more aggressive approach to selling them.

A range of coloured shoes was launched, incorporating new materials such as EVA and a Union Jack trademark, while the company's name was changed from Foster & Son to Reebok – that of a small South African deer, noted for its grace and fleetness of foot.

From their base in Bolton the Foster family began looking to the export market, and in the 1970s their products caught the eye of the American entrepreneur, Paul Fireman, who wanted to challenge Nike for control of the booming market in running shoes.

It was the start of a rivalry which has lasted to the present day, and continues to dominate the sportswear industry in the same way that the celebrated 'cola wars' have been played out in a different field of commerce.

WE'VE COME A LONG WAY, BABY . . .

Reebok has come a million miles from those pioneering days to reach its present status as one of the world's top makers of sports footwear and clothing. Nowadays our products adorn the feet of street-wise youngsters and Hollywood stars as well as Olympic sportsmen and women, and tremendous resources are applied in the never-ending pursuit of technical excellence.

Yet the lessons of the past help to explain the ways in which Reebok has developed from those early days in the north of England, and the challenges which we have set ourselves for the coming era of unparalleled global expansion.

US BUSINESS GROWTH PAVES THE WAY FOR THE REST OF THE WORLD

When Paul Fireman set out to launch Reebok in the USA, his inspiration was to produce the most comfortable athletic shoe ever worn, using pliable and lightweight materials, such as garment leather in the construction. This coincided with the beginning of the aerobic boom in California, where it was reported that women were exercising in bare feet.

The result was the Freestyle, a women's aerobic shoe which rapidly established itself as a design classic, combining softness and flexibility with a distinctive white colour scheme and an unusual puckered effect on the toe (actually a production fault); just as a great chef blends simple ingredients to create a recipe of genius.

No money was available for marketing but the product was launched in the early 1980s, just as the aerobics boom was sweeping the USA. Demand for the Freestyle spread like wildfire, and it was soon adopted by the smart young businesswomen and secretaries of Wall Street as a symbol of their freedom from the slavery of high-heeled shoes.

So it came about that the brand exploded into mass popularity across the Atlantic as a fashion statement and even a symbol of women's growing independence.

Naturally Reebok was keen to exploit this grassroots popularity, but in a way which also stressed the product's merits as a serious performance shoe. The result was the Aerobic Instructor's Alliance, a network with 40,000 members across America who taught while wearing the Reebok product.

In this way the company forged a powerful and long-lasting connection with the women's fitness community, first in the USA and later throughout the world, which fuelled a massive surge in Reebok's fortunes from $60 million in sales in 1982 to $1 billion in 1986.

By now Reebok was the hottest stock on Wall Street, seizing the number one spot from Nike and buying out the original British operation, which henceforth became a subsidiary and the base for activities outside the USA.

EXPANSION BEYOND THE US BEGINS

But despite this phenomenal expansion in the USA, there were clearly further hurdles to be cleared. Firstly, the company's operation outside North America remained comparatively small scale and fragmented, with sales in the rest of the world totalling less than $100 million – just one-tenth of the US figure in 1986.

Secondly, although Reebok was already moving successfully into the basketball and tennis markets, the brand's appeal had to be widened by building up its following in a further range of sports and physical activities.

Reebok has responded to these challenges with a vision which has already turned the company into a major global player, and now points the way towards our declared goal of becoming the world's number one sports and fitness brand by 1996.

THE CHALLENGE OF BUILDING A BRAND

When I joined Reebok five years ago, during a series of top-level changes which brought in professional managers from a range of business sectors, the chairman of my previous company told me that I was crazy to go off and sell shoes.

My reply was that I was leaving to develop and market one of the world's great brand names. In my view enhancing and reinforcing that brand image, both on and off the sports field, has been, and will continue to be, the key to Reebok's enduring success.

GLOBAL EXPANSION CONTINUES

Our never-ending search for new areas of sporting enterprise has gone hand in hand with the expansion of our activities throughout the world. A total of 47 countries are now covered by Reebok's network of distributors and subsidiaries, with our products on sale in 110 countries.

The upshot of this expansion has been that in 1992, Reebok's international arm reached its target of $1 billion, making it roughly 40 per cent of the size of the US operation. That proportion could well rise to as much as 60 per cent within the next two years.

Fascinating opportunities have been thrown up by the freeing of eastern Europe, and we recently opened Moscow's first totally dedicated athletic footwear and sportswear shop, with takings of $200,000 in the first week alone. Reebok has shown its commitment to this expanding market by signing a contract to sponsor the Russian Athletic Federation in all events leading up to the next Olympic Games.

TECHNICAL INNOVATION

The primary stage in maintaining the brand's reputation for excellence is clearly technical innovation. For instance, we revolutionised basketball with the legendary Pump™ system, which supports the player's foot in an inflatable cushion of air – creating in the process, in just 18 months, a retail business worth $750 million in the USA. This breakthrough is now being applied to a whole new range of products including running and tennis footwear and even cycling helmets.

Our multi-faceted approach embraces a number of further technologies, including Insta-Pump™, a more advanced pump concept giving customised support on the upper as well as through the midsole to offer further support to high performance athletes.

We have also developed Hexalite™, a honeycomb-structured substance to provide cushioning, and a carbon fibre material called Graphlite™ which is used to make a strong but lightweight sole.

Having developed these technologies, we need to communicate their benefits to consumers, both in the world of sport and beyond, and clearly advertising has a positive part to play in establishing Reebok as a leader in this field.

Reebok reached its target of $1 billion sales in the USA by spending only $10 million a year on advertising. Admittedly that figure has since rocketed as the market has matured, and by the time we reached $1.5 billion our advertising spend – along with that of our major competitors – had increased tenfold.

TOTAL DEDICATION TO SPORT

A crucial factor in sustaining Reebok's long-term success has been our continuing involvement in sport at all levels, from back-street basketball competitions such as the 'Blacktop Euro 3 on 3' to the Olympic Games. Around 10 per cent of our advertising and marketing budget goes on sponsorship of this kind, and over the years it has proved to be a wise investment.

For the brand to maintain its credibility, our products must be seen as the choice of top athletes, helping them to push back the boundaries of sporting prowess.

At the Barcelona Olympics a number of track and field athletes were willing to stake their reputations on Reebok by competing in what was virtually a prototype of the Insta-Pump™ shoe. Their faith was rewarded with a total of five medals. Admittedly there are also risks for us in backing even the world's most renowned athletes. Our campaign surrounding the American decathletes

Dave Johnson and Dan O'Brien hit a setback when Dan failed to qualify for the Olympics – though even this was turned to best advantage by clever use of advertising.

There are, however, countless examples of world-famous sportsmen and women whose achievements have reflected glory on the brand, for instance tennis stars Michael Chang, Michael Stich and Arantxa Sanchez, who all flourish under our sponsorship.

In the US National Basketball Association, no less than 30 per cent of the players wear Reebok, including the hottest prospect of all, Shaquille O'Neal, who towers over the game not just physically (at seven feet one inch tall) but also in terms of his promise as one of the world's top sporting stars. Shaquille was voted NBA Rookie of the Year for 1993.

WHY THE SUPPORT OF ATHLETES IS SO IMPORTANT

The backing of leading athletes helps to create respect and 'attitude' for the brand – a crucial factor in the eyes of consumers, who are typically young men and women in the 13–20 bracket. But there is another, equally important strand to our sponsorship strategy, which may be termed grassroots marketing.

This involves providing support for local teams and sporting clubs, sponsoring small-town competitions and tournaments, and generally forging links with young amateurs and future professionals which will endure throughout their careers.

One example of this imaginative approach is our backing for inner-city basketball, played on outdoor tarmac or 'blacktop' courts, and tied in with a specially designed range of products. Associated with this is a programme for refurbishing run-down or vandalised basketball courts, enabling us to give something back to the community with which we do business.

Similarly our long-running connection with aerobics has prospered, and we have breathed new life into the activity with an entirely new exercise programme called Step Reebok^{TM}, a total body workout that involves stepping on and off an adjustable platform. Again we have taken the trouble to cultivate grassroots support with a network of 70,000 instructors and a range of other promotional activities.

AND NOW SOCCER

The same painstaking approach has been applied as we have widened our horizons to embrace more and more sports and physical activities. Our growing involvement in soccer – the world's most popular sport – has been stimulated by sponsoring top European players and by promoting events for youngsters such as Reebok Fives Street Soccer, the biggest five-a-side tournament of its kind in Europe.

. . . AND BEYOND

Our new Bodywalk™ programme capitalises on the enormous popularity of walking as a fitness activity, while the boom in outdoor pursuits such as rock-climbing and mountain-biking has pointed the way to another major area for commercial expansion in the near future.

We have responded to worldwide concerns about the environment by introducing an environmentally friendly shoe, its uppers made of organically tanned leather, its soles from recycled car tyres.

HUMAN RIGHTS

Perhaps unusually for a multinational firm, we have outspokenly pledged ourselves to the cause of human rights, with a series of co-operative ventures with Amnesty International and the establishment of our own human rights foundation. As part of the foundation, an annual award is given to young people who make a significant contribution to the promotion of human rights in their country. This commitment has not been deflected by our own commercial interests, and a human rights award was recently made to a campaigner imprisoned by the government of Indonesia, a country where up to 20 per cent of our products are manufactured.

THE SYNERGIES BUILD THE BRAND

These wide-ranging activities, diverse in themselves, fit together like pieces of a jigsaw to create Reebok's image as a brand which is both aspirational and inspirational, passionate and compassionate, aimed at fun-lovers and serious contenders alike.

It is a concept summed up in a single but all-embracing slogan: *Planet Reebok*. This is a world which individual sportsmen and women, whether amateur or professional, can fulfil their own potential through application and dedication. Above all, it is a world in which they can leap over any obstacle to realise their dreams.

OUR STRATEGY FOR THE FUTURE

We now face a future which presents greater opportunities than ever before, but which also demands that we harness our commercial power in the most effective way, by combining the creativity of an artist with the discipline of a true athlete.

To this end we shall move increasingly towards the creation of a truly global brand, delivering common advertising and marketing themes to ensure a recognisable identity for our products in every country where they are sold.

At the same time we tread a delicate line, remembering that sport and fashion vary from country to country, and ensuring that scope remains for creativity on the part of our general managers, whose entrepreneurial flair has been responsible for building the brand's success in their own countries.

'THINK GLOBAL, ACT LOCAL'

I believe that the ideal compromise will be strong local management working within a clearly defined global framework, in which the overall direction of the brand is firmly established. This approach contrasts starkly with that of our main competitors, who prefer to concentrate power in the hands of an increasingly strong central management.

Too much is at stake for there to be any let-up in the commercial struggle between Reebok and Nike. Over the years we have tended to dominate the world of women's fitness, while their greatest strength has been in men's sport. Both of us are now determined to seize the other's territory; ultimately only one of us can succeed.

As the battle progresses, it will demand many changes in the structure of our business. Sophisticated information systems will help us to monitor sales in a more detailed way. Production, which for at least a decade has been carried out by sub-contractors in the Far East, may well return to Europe and the USA.

The production of sports clothing is likely to become ever more important, and could expand from 20 per cent of our business at present to around 50 per cent in the future.

Meanwhile the support of retailers will also be a vital factor, raising the question of how far Reebok should go in setting up its own chain of retail outlets – a step which would alter the entire financial profile of the company.

No one can predict exactly how the company will evolve to meet the coming challenges. But as long as we remain sensitive to the demands of the marketplace, listening to the messages which come to us from the street and the sports field, and responding with energy and excitement, then the sun will continue to shine on Planet Reebok.

John Duerden

John Duerden, 52, first joined Reebok in October 1988 as MD and COO of the company's International Division headquarters in Bolton, England.

Duerden was placed in charge of Reebok's global operations as President of Reebok Worldwide in February 1990. He was named CEO and elected to the Board of Directors of Reebok International Limited in June 1991.

In August 1992, Duerden was appointed President of Reebok International Division, responsible for international operations.

Prior to joining Reebok, he worked for 20 years for the Xerox Corporation in a variety of corporate and international marketing management positions. His last position there was VP of Business Development. Previously he was Director of Operations for all Rank Xerox operations outside western Europe.

Born in Wales, he was educated in the UK where he was an amateur rugby player. He is an avid runner and sailor.

Reebok International Ltd

Reebok International Ltd is one of the world's leading designers, marketers and distributors of sports, fitness and lifestyle products. The company's brands in Europe include Reebok Rockport, AVIA and BOKS. Total worldwide sales of the company's products in 1992 totalled $3.02 billion.

Reebok products are sold in about 140 countries, through a network of subsidiary companies and independent distributors. It is one of the leading sports brands throughout Europe and the number one brand in the UK, Spain and Denmark. The company is also expanding rapidly in the emerging markets of central and eastern Europe.

Reebok's international division relocated to Stockley Park, near London's Heathrow Airport, in 1993.

Index

accountability 75
acquisitions 21
advertising strategy 33, 66, 72
ally development 21
Andersen Consulting 9, 81–95
apparel, sporting 133–43
Asia 60, 98
Australia 47, 52, 108
Austria 41
automatic teller machines 102
automation 7

barriers, trade 8, 61, 82, 97, 98
Belgium 22, 31, 41, 43, 66, 69, 103
brands 8, 21, 64, 72, 133–7, 140–1
Burson-Marsteller Europe 8, 21–9, 66
business school 25, 116

Campbell Biscuits Europe 9, 63–70
Canada 100, 101, 108, 118
cashless society 103
cause marketing 21
central Europe 11–20, 74
change 7, 21, 26, 45, 60, 63, 81–5, 112–13 117, 121, 122–3, 124
chemicals 8, 11–20
choice, customer 33
communications 9, 17, 21–9, 67, 98, 112, 114, 115, 116
communications and public affairs 8, 21–9
community relations 21
competitiveness 12, 24, 82, 89
computers 8, 31–41
consultancy 21, 81, 88

continuous improvement 7, 91
contract catering 8, 43–52
contracting out 44, 45, 49
cost effectiveness 44, 55, 126
cost reduction 12, 75, 125
courier services 9, 53–62
credo, corporate 109
crisis management/preparedness 21
cross-border 8, 22, 23, 97, 98, 103
cultural differences 100–1
culture, corporate 48, 49, 122, 127
customer focus 75, 84, 142
Customs 53, 57–8
cyclical markets 123
Czech Republic 13, 22, 38

delayering, management 7
Denmark 22
DHL Worldwide Express 9, 53–62
differentiation 35, 97
divestiture 12, 63, 67
Du Pont de Nemours International SA 8, 11–20
Duerden, John 133, 143

eastern Europe 11–20, 43, 60, 74, 101, 137
economies of scale 50, 72
Ellis, Vernon 81, 94
empowerment 48
environment 12, 18, 53, 56–7, 87, 101, 112, 122, 127, 140
ergonomics 35
European Community 11, 15, 56, 57, 58, 97, 98, 102, 103

European Economic Area 11
expectations, customer 7, 59, 60, 75, 82

facilities management 43, 50–1, 88
Far East 47, 52, 142
feudal structure 23
fifth-freedom rights 56
financial communications 21
financial incentives 15
flexibility 7, 13, 24, 27, 31, 127
Food & Drug Administration 110, 115
foods 9, 63–70
foreign aid 15
foreign exchange 102
Forte PLC 9, 52, 71–9
Forte, Rocco 71, 78
France 31, 41, 43, 45, 66, 68, 69, 73, 79, 100, 101
franchising 38

Gardner Merchant Services Group 8, 43–52, 72
Germany 22, 31, 37, 38, 39, 41, 43, 45, 47, 66, 68, 69, 79, 101, 103, 108
global strategy 7, 8, 9, 16, 47, 114, 137, 141
global village 98
globalisation 8, 12, 55, 60, 103, 141
government relations 21
grassroots marketing 139
Greece 38
greenfield sites 18
growth management 53, 54

harmonisation 8, 58, 60, 82
Hawkes, Garry 43, 52
health-care communications 23
home banking 104
hotels and restaurants 9
human rights 140
Hungary 13, 22

IBM 31, 32, 33, 124–5
image 9, 87, 107, 110, 141
information technology 9, 81–95
infrastructure 13, 14, 44, 77, 101, 104
internal communications 21
inventories 55, 60
inventory control 32, 33
investment 11, 14–15, 49, 55, 60, 63, 67, 104, 123, 129
investor relations 21, 111
Ireland 43, 79
ISO 9000 38, 89
issue management 23
Italy 22, 31, 41, 43, 73, 108

Japan 52, 83, 118
job creation 15
job security 12
joint ventures 12
just-in time delivery 8, 55, 60, 83, 128

kaizen 7, 83
knowledge capital 92
Kuijpers, Robert M 53, 62

language skills 47
Lieven, Theo 31, 40
Lindheim, James B 21, 28
Lipton, Stuart 121, 130
long-term commitment 16
Luxembourg 31, 41

Maastricht 82
management buyout 49, 72
market economy 13, 16, 18
market expertise 13
marketing 25, 75, 97, 98, 99, 116, 139
marketing communications 21, 23
mass market 34
media relations 24, 87
Mexico 100

Middle East 52, 79
mission, corporate 21, 67, 87, 90, 111, 113
Moerk, Edward 5 63, 69
motivation, employee 21
multi-domestic 100
multinational 22, 27, 64, 89, 93, 100
multiskilling 7, 75

Netherlands 22, 31, 41, 43, 45, 47, 66, 69, 108
networking 23, 25, 63, 84
networks 23, 53, 67, 74, 139
new world order 15
niche marketing 8, 24
North America 47, 52, 60, 73, 79, 136
North American Free Trade Agreement 98
North Sea 45, 124
notebook computer 32–3, 36–7

Olympic Games 137, 138–9
outsourcing 7, 91

Pacific rim 15
pan-Europe 64, 65, 66, 67, 73, 97
paradigms 88–93
partnering 8, 9, 83, 90, 115, 128
payment systems 9, 97–106
performance-related awards 75
personal digital assistant 36–7
pharmaceuticals 9, 49, 107–119
planning 16, 126
Poland 13, 22, 31, 41, 73
political upheaval 13
Portugal 38, 103
practices 23
price cutting 23
private enterprise 13
privatisation 21, 82
product development 26
professional relations 110

profitability 12, 55, 63, 67, 74, 126
property 9, 121–31
public affairs 21–9, 114
public relations 21, 24, 66, 110
publicity 21

quality 25, 38, 44, 49, 75, 114, 122, 127

R&D 49, 119
rationalisation, corporate 7, 64, 84
real estate 9, 121–31
recession 23, 74, 76, 128
recycling 55, 84
Reebok International 9, 133–43
reengineering, organisational 7, 84, 85, 89, 90
regulations 8, 14, 53, 56, 77, 110, 111
relationships, customer 7, 8, 32, 90, 124
reorganisation, business 23, 67, 72
research 34, 47, 68, 90, 107, 112, 113, 119, 123, 125
resource management 55, 126
restructuring 12, 84
risk 14, 21, 128
Russell, Charles T 97, 105
Russia 13, 137

sales training 21
Scandinavia 22, 38
scholarships 17
seamlessness 23, 59, 91–2
service improvements 53, 58–9
simplification 7, 8, 12
single market 23, 84
SmithKline Beecham PLC 9, 107–19
social contract 109, 110, 114
social partnership 13
South America 52, 98
Spain 22, 31, 41, 43, 103
sponsorship 138–9

sporting apparel 9
standardisation 8, 60
Stanhope Properties PLC 9, 121–31
state-run economic system 13
Switzerland 22, 31, 41

target pricing 124
teamwork 48
technology 7, 17, 53, 60, 76, 82, 85, 89, 90, 95, 103, 112, 122
telecommunications 101
trade associations 111, 112, 113
trade relations 21
training 21, 26, 49
transmigration 22
transnationalism 27
transparency 9, 103
trends 36, 55, 75, 76, 97–8, 126
Turkey 38

UK 22, 38, 43, 44–5, 49, 50, 51, 69, 73, 79, 82, 92, 100, 108, 110, 119, 123, 128
USA 17, 20, 22, 69, 99, 101, 102, 107, 108, 110, 117, 128, 133, 135, 136, 138, 142

value 12, 44, 49, 82, 87, 107, 122, 123, 126, 127, 128
value added 56, 128
value-added tax 58
value-based pricing 24, 90
values 49, 81, 83, 114
video conferencing 76
Visa International 9, 97–106
vision, corporate 9, 64–5, 87, 101, 106
Vobis Microcomputer AG 8, 31–41

Wendt, Henry 107, 118
western Europe 51, 60
western governments 14–15
Williamson, David V S 11, 19
win/win 8, 83, 90